Chosen Vessel

(Purpose/ Poverty/ Prosperity)

S. R. Sampson.

Scripture taken from the King James Version of the Bible.

WestBow Press books may be ordered through booksellers or by contacting:

WestBow Press
A Division of Thomas Nelson & Zondervan
1663 Liberty Drive
Bloomington, IN 47403
www.westbowpress.com
1 (866) 928-1240

ISBN: 978-1-5127-4640-2 (sc)
ISBN: 978-1-5127-4639-6 (e)

Library of Congress Control Number: 2016909999

Print information available on the last page.

WestBow Press rev. date: 12/29/2016

Contents

Introduction

Chosen Vessel, realistically all that breath life is chosen; God chose to create and therefore, has a plan for all life. If you think about it within the youthful years of life, you look forward to the opportunity of being chosen by your mom to complete a task, and in grade school when your teacher chose you as a helper or to play a part in a play you are elated with excitement because you are the chosen one to complete the task. You view it as a privilege, an opportunity! As a youth, most views it as a delight to be chosen, when given the opportunity you feel special that your teacher, parents, minister or friend; chose you for the challenge or a special role. As the chosen vessel, the challenge of who, when and why is answered? You exhibit the traits, talents and gifts to get the job done.

Exactly as we are selected to be the chosen vessel from our teacher(s) in school or parents; in the same manner we can become God's chosen vessels, God works through people on earth! God chose each individual to complete His divine work. God, The Teacher, has chosen you, as our maker he divinely equips you to master the plans that's he has set! God established the plan and in this book focuses on submitting, securing and/or meeting the needs of every creature. God the creator desires that no one goes without the things needed. The gifts that he has given, abilities and talents are how He completes this task, inclusively. In Chosen Vessel, an introduction is given on how God deals with the gift of giving, a plan to cast out poverty, and just how to use ones given purpose, to reach an equilibrium. All should taste prosperity in one way or another; sometimes personally or through family or friends. Yet, it is a must that the alignment of God's Word is completed, incorporating his plan into our lives. As we see God first. Yes, most enter the world with less and eventually increase – as sleep befalls upon every man--- your purpose, -- is the key to prosperity --- and to an extraordinary life.

Dedication or Tribune – Honoring

Tammy Nnamoni – A special friend who provided advice and guidance, and always shared the challenges of life.

Anjelica - My Sweet Daughter who sacrificed as she dealt with the challenges of life. Love and Grace beholds as Beauty shines through her, truly she is a Child of God.

Father Sampson, Senior – Who's sight has declined and can never actually read this book, but yet with hope, will know/hear of its existence and progress.

CHAPTER 1

SHORT TESTIMONY

Chosen Vessel

Chosen Vessel, is written to inspire the plans of God for humankind to live in harmony as all recognize the plans of God. God has implemented a plan to take care of all people and to minister to their needs as the end times of this life on the earth transitions, changing the dynamics of life as we know it today. God has a plan to aid in various aspects of these changing times so that all people will have what they need. He will help them grow and prosper during the upcoming end of days, the study of which is known as *eschatology,* the study and confirmation of what will occur during the last days, known by many as the "end times, the final events noted in scripture that will occur before the return of the messiah.

The last days are upon us, and the change of the way we live on earth as we know it will occur for all existing people. God has proclaimed that governments and the Anti-Christ will control the world, and that all should prepare. As God has His chosen vessels providing leadership and other vessels to assist, all should adhere to the needs of their neighbors. So how and why did this book come about? As I was new in my studies, and exploring the Word of God, upon obtaining new knowledge, and at the end of my weekly Bible study, I stood in the foyer of the church's training center and I heard a whisper, a steady voice of clarity. Yet, it was an audible voice in a soft whisper, which said, "I desire that you teach." I believe that is very close to the words that I heard. Maybe it wasn't the words verbatim, but needless to say, I was in such a state of disbelief that the exact words escapes me at this time. The gist was that He desired that I teach and not to confuse the matter. I was in His house, which meant to me that I needed to teach the Word. I could not believe that I heard the voice of God and that He actually took the time to speak to me!

As a few weeks passed, I began trying to comprehend exactly how I would go about teaching. I gathered the pieces together, in my mind, of what the role of teaching meant. Honestly, I did not know what steps to take. Several months later, in February 2014, I was told in a prophecy that I would write a book. As for the title or the subject matter, I had no clue. That is how the birth of this book began.

As I waited for God to reveal all that He had planned, I tried to prepare myself for the walk that I had before me. I enhanced my prayer life and established a deeper relationship with the Father. In addition, I wanted to invest time in serving, so I volunteered and joined two ministries. I did not realize how much I did not know until I began to invest time in studying scripture. I was now an active church member, but the knowledge that I had was not enough to teach anyone. I thought I had the basic knowledge, yet I was awakened to the fact that the Bible was unlike any other book. The history, prophecies, and revelations of truth would be hard to comprehend without extensive studies. Biblical knowledge would require an investment of time, and the need to focus on studies. For God had summoned me!

As I concentrate on studies, I spent continuous hours reading and seeking to learn. One evening as night fell, I lay down to rest, yet I was physically restless, awaiting sleep. I began to think about how anxious I felt, and that I needed to learn; I desire to learn as much as possible, as soon as possible. I was on a journey, filled with the Holy Spirit and the Word of God, and it felt wonderful! As I lay awake, I decided to pray; it was a way to escape and release all to God. So I began, "Heavenly Father ..." and then releasing it all, slowly my voice began to fade as sleep fell upon me. As I came to an end, I said "amen" and fell to sleep. However, I suddenly found myself rolling over. It had to have been two or three o'clock in the morning, and abruptly I started fumbling around, looking for paper and pen. I heard a voice, a whisper that whispered these words: "For what you do for the least of these, you have done for me."

> *And the King shall answer and say unto them, Verily I say unto you, Inasmuch as ye have done it unto one of the least of these my brethren, ye have done it unto me,* (Matthew 25:40, KJV).

I knew this would be the subject of the book that God petitioned me to write, I just Knew! I made a note, of Matthew 25:40, the subject reference scripture—this was the start! This was it!

As I gathered the information, studied, and received revelation of the subject material, each heading and expression began to flow. I came to an understanding of why this was the subject of discussion. The Holy Spirit revealed additional information to me. I received the book's provision in October or November 2014. So as you go forth with your reading, this book is the Word of God, God desires all to understand. Inspired by God,—Enjoy!

Chapter 2

Chosen Vessel

Purpose — Poverty — Prosperity

In reading you are given a perspective, an opportunity to truly look at where we stand in faith. Being chosen as a vessel is honestly how we discern the use of the gift(s) God has given. We have been chosen with a purpose to perceive and to help others, even give financially. Supporting the needs of others is a privilege and a gift. Every season (and the success thereof) determines the next chapter in the new season ahead. I desire to cover the need to look at money, people, God, and the distributions of God's money in a new perspective of giving. God's blessings are available to all. Of course it is senseless for me to say that God owns everything.

God spoke into existence all that exists; therefore, He is the ***maker*** and ***producer*** of all things. He provides humankind with the creativity to develop new inventions; must I say every idea and every invention, *all* came from the Master Creator, the heavenly Father of the universe. God embedded in the minds and in the hearts of humans the ideas for the creation of computers, automobiles, houses, and airplanes. Yes, the credit goes to Him! God, through humankind, demonstrates His power and purpose on this earth through the selection of His gifts and the operation of His chosen vessels. As growth transforms and miracles happen, God is glorified!

Sincerely, I confess that many believe they are privileged to have special talents and gifts because they are "gifted" and they are "good," and with hard work the manifestation of that talent now exists. Yes, they have worked hard to train, study, and advance, and all recognitions and rewards are earned out of perseverance, commitment, and dedication to the task. Yet God's touch has been completely overlooked. Remember, God gave you all of your abilities. God made you, God chose you, and He chose to open the door to prosperity. The door to your success is God's success! Your success is for His Glory, and He has a plan in all of it. He has a plan for each creation, for everything and everyone, and for all seasons in everything that He creates. God plants the seed, whether it is an individual of poverty or prosperity; ultimately, God has a plan that He will manifest.

Perseverance and faith provide you the victory of successfully going through each level of promotion, and God is the promoter. It is God's purpose and His life plan. God's design is in your purpose, and it is carved into every individual. We must stand in faith as He completes His work, not only for us, but through us as He uses each of us to touch, ignite, and cultivate others. The rotation of His cycle turns as He completes the work He sets forth. Our purpose and His plan to help us prosper is the ultimate goal that enhances our lives and eliminates poverty, and there is only one direction in which God has laid out gifts to maintain perfect balance in the world.

How does God's plans fall together, and how can we learn to stand and wait during each season as He develops each one for His presence we must listen, wait and obey. We must align our lives with God, since God works in cycles, washing, teaching, and blessing. As we all sin and fall short, we are constantly confessing our sins as we desire to stay close to God and to receive His direction in our lives. As we become polished in the talents and gifts that we possess, we move forth and enhance our skills. As we fill up, we go out performing at greater levels, therefore; we work at higher levels, knowing that we are now prepared to perform at our best.

> *In the day of prosperity be joyful, but in the day of adversity consider: God also hath set the one over against the other, to the end that man should find nothing after him,* (Ecclesiastes 7:14, KJV).

Why does God allow trials to come upon us as we are equipped to take on challenges and perform at levels that we have never performed before? God has high expectations and has equipped us to rise and continue to escalate. We all go through trials, which could mean periods of promotions to higher levels of faith, striving to reach an extraordinary level of success. Yes, faith and obedience are required, during these periods, and sometimes our income will fluctuate. Trials are only periods of times when our faith is tested. We build and take on new challenges, and new learning takes place, moving us to new heights.

God has equipped us all to reach an equilibrium point and rise to a level of success. As we mature in our walk, we learn and grow, reaching back to teach others to manifest and continue on their journey. As time goes on, we will reach retirement. If we have children or young progressive individual influences, we disciple them so they are positioned to follow as youthful leaders, and God's work continues (such in the case of Moses and Joshua) As we stand in His presence His blessing are upon us, as we listen and walk in faith. The vessels that we are, we will acknowledge the almighty God and submit to His calling.

Chapter 3

VESSEL of Purpose

(FAITH)

God's blessing are received His children, in each season, which given to Manifest growth; emotionally, financially and spiritually. God has a plan for each of his children, and knows who will prosper. For God has predestined each one of us and has plans set for us. He will lead us according to his plans.

Why are many of God's children financially crippled, leaning on society and the help of the wealthy to cover the basic necessities of life? God has plans of developing, teaching, growing, and placing us in different seasons, requiring that each humbles themselves. Humility is part of God's plan, and there are many other reasons God have placed individuals in seasons of low income or hardship. Our job is to do what we can to help when the call is placed before us.

The distribution of money is used as a teacher, a blessing. Many would ask, how is the lack of money used to teach? Poverty humbles. It brings an understanding of God's will, for all of His people. Poverty opens our eyes to the repercussion of the life of lower income, and it teaches compassion and love. Many never reach a high level of understanding because many never experience a level of poverty. A level of understanding is reached with experience and a different outlook or mindset is realized. Each level of growth provides a new level of understanding, and can be used to Glorify God. As a chosen vessel, the productive and creative growth provides appreciation of His blessings, regardless of how small, providing thanksgiving and the desire to give back into the lives of others.

Therefore, what is one of God's main goals? To love our neighbor as we love ourselves, (Deuteronomy 6:6). God desires that we feel the need of others, that we pray for one another; that we reach out and give our neighbor a helping hand. Does the closing or opening of the door to a life of hardship provide assistance in understanding the life of a poor man? Yes, it does! Yet wealth is a blessing, and should always be appreciated.

To extend a hand is to provide the evidences of God's love and adored mercy of our lives. The love and the extending of love to others is a gift, a commandment that is stated as one of the two main commands that God desires man to always honor; Mark 12:31. How, who, or when do we let go and help others by giving and sharing? God blesses people through others, and regardless if anyone would like to admit, **ALL IS HIS, AND COMES FROM HIM.** ***God chose to bless. God has a purpose, and as He selects individuals as "Vessels," for each given task, so that the purpose, the plan that He has on the earth will be complete.***

Romans 8:28–30, (KJV)

> 28 And we know that all things work together for good to them that love God, to them who are the called according to his purpose.
>
> 29 For whom he did foreknow, he also did predestinate to be conformed to the image of his Son, that he might be the firstborn among many brethren.

<u>God Gives</u>

God gives life as well as blessings. Life is a wonder, a beautiful gift that God has given. We, as faithful recipients, receive all gifts including the gift of financial success. This is also a blessing that God freely gives. All gifts, if we sincerely think about it, are free and are given by God, FREELY, yet it glorifies God. Remember, He too gives love unconditionally.

Our lives are Gifts. The body is magnificent. The body is formed with all organs working together and functioning in sync, glorifying the creator, perfectly designed. The heart is only one of the many organs, which pumps blood throughout the body and symbolically demonstrates love as we depict the illustration in books, magazines, and cards to express love. Love is a free gift, and the heart is an extraordinary organ; God's love flows, redemption and grace comes freely as the heart, symbolically grows closer to God.

Each one of our organs given by God demonstrates how He connects all things together in unity, working together as one body to reach a common cause. God's plan involves unity, the demonstration of love. God presents love first through His son, and set the example of ultimate sacrifice by demonstrating love for man, giving His son as the redeemer for the sin of mankind. God gives the gift of salvation, the gift of life. FREELY

None of us has earned the gift of life, BUT IT WAS GIVEN TO US. It is all a gift from God. All creation is a gift of God. None of us can earn that, if we think we have earned it, we are mistaken. We underestimate what God has given us. The world itself and all the blessings that are in the earth, God gave to every living soul. Our abilities and everything we have are gifts from God. God desires that we give to one another and love each other as He (God) set the example.

Please, do not look at a man's financial status, nationality, gender, mental capacity, or educational level, and pre-determine what he is worthy of in this life; or what he can achieve! The power of success befalls on the Lord, and He will take that man, child, or woman, despite skills or status, to whatever level He desires. No man achieves without the hand of God. It is God, and only God who manifests success. We must all stand in knowledge that it is God's purpose and God's prosperity! Yes, it is a valuable realization to grasp, that it is all given at no cost, it is FREE!

Look at life as it is, the true treasure that we have received through Christ, the Lord, our Savior. Christ, who offers the gift of salvation. It is the greatest gift we can receive.

As you have been given, in return, give gifts freely, and in return it will afford you God's extended promises, His blessings, His Favor.

And in Psalm, we must know that financial support should be given to those who are in need, as we read:

Proverbs 22:16, (KJV)

> 16 He that oppresseth the poor to increase his riches, and he that giveth to the rich, shall surely come to want.

God's Plan – Supply of Food to Every Living Thing

The gift of Stewardship is not an easy role, but financial success extends from us to provide a helping hand to others. In return, others will provide a hand to another, moving forward to another set of hands, and progressing one individual at a time and/or every family, uniting all households and the community.

God uses people to provide for each other. This is His plan. He has a plan to feed the birds by providing a food supply. He has a plan to feed such animals as the hawk, which preys on other birds. The coyotes and wolves prey on chipmunks or other crawling animals as their source of food. In the sea, sea animals, fish, and whales find food in their habitat. Each has plenty, more than enough food in their environment, and the food chain continues. Yes, God provides a food chain for all creation. Man is considered to be the highest level of creation. He aides in taking care of the needs of his own, feeding his household, as well as extending food to other creatures. It is all part of God's earthly plan and should not be overlooked.

God rewards generous giving, and has petitioned and gifted individuals with increased income to accommodate other people in need. In fact, God knows that many will be incapable of managing their own money, and therefore, would need keen people with mathematical or financial management skills to assist. God has made provisions, and both giver and taker should submit.

Receive Not

It is true that many do not know how to receive. Being that all belongs to God, when a gift is given, it should be accepted. Receive with thanksgiving, knowing that God has supplied. Do not be concerned with paying a gift back in any shape or form, but just receive it! God blesses abundantly, and therefore, we should become givers. He will tug on our hearts when it is time and the need is there. Each time we give, we should give freely, and without the expectation of payback. God provides and replenishes. The wealth of the land is the Lord's.

Whatever it takes to receive the gift of salvation supersedes any accumulation of wealth. What do we value, is it Salvation? Are we called upon to give? The Gift of Giving falls upon ALL BELIEVERS, whether it is time, money, knowledge, or any service. All are freely given to us by God, therefore; should be freely given to others, which means that a seed is planted and as seeds are planted continue growth will occur. Sincerely it is part of the walk as the chosen vessel of the Lord. We should receive with thanksgiving and give with thanks that we are chosen to help in the role as the servant. We should know that God will continue to supply, to the receiver and to the giver, Jehovah Jireh, the provider.

Be The Light **— Jehovah Jireh**

God has many reasons why He allows us to be subjected to periods of low income. As a people, always lend a compassionate heart and know that God is at work.

As some are truly favored and gifted; provided through the blessings of God, how or why are some privileged with so much, while others seem to wander through life just barely making ends meet? Many are unable to excel, as simple vacations or travels create a financial hardship. The ability to rise above the mediocre of meeting the monthly bills of the household is so very difficult. How can we justify that even the children of God are NOT ALL OVERFLOWING IN WEALTH AND PROSPERITY?

God is a loving Father, for He provides financial growth and prosperity to everyone. In order to receive the blessings of God, we go through preparation that advances us through to each level of promotion, while others are born with financial success. God creates the plan. God guides and teaches, and prospers each of us on different economic levels.

Believe it or not, trials occur as we walk the Christian walk to serve and live as Christians. There will be times when money may be scarce, and we will need to reach out to the community for help. People need people, and during hard times, as established people of financial security are summoned to help others, God provides the gift of prosperity to be the light as a source to others in such times of need. When we see a need, and we have an overflow, whether it is cash, clothes, shelter, or food, as God's children, as noted in the scriptures, we should be willing to provide. The doors should be open to the needs of the community, as in the light to brighten darkness. We all should show the love and compassion of God in all that we do. God established a plan for His Glory through chosen vessels, of which He provides evidences of His Love for the World. **To give is only one way; He shines light to bring awareness of His love.**

God uses people as the Vessels to carry out or supply the needs to others; note the verses below:

1 John 3:16–24, (KJV)

> 16 Hereby perceive we the love of God, because he laid down his life for us: and we ought to lay down our lives for the brethren.
>
> 17 But whoso hath this world's good, and seeth his brother have need, and shutteth up his bowels of compassion from him, how dwelleth the love of God in him?
>
> 18 My little children, let us not love in word, neither in tongue; but in deed and in truth.
>
> 19 And hereby we know that we are of the truth, and shall assure our hearts before him.
>
> 20 For if our heart condemn us, God is greater than our heart, and knoweth all things.
>
> 21 Beloved, if our heart condemn us not, then have we confidence toward God.
>
> 22 And whatsoever we ask, we receive of him, because we keep his commandments, and do those things that are pleasing in his sight.
>
> 23 And this is his commandment, That we should believe on the name of his Son Jesus Christ, and love one another, as he gave us commandment.

[24] And he that keepeth his commandments dwelleth in him, and he in him. And hereby we know that he abideth in us, by the Spirit which he hath given us.

Version (KJV)

And note the scriptures in James:

James 2:14–17, (KJV)

[14] What doth it profit, my brethren, though a man say he hath faith, and have not works? can faith save him?

[15] If a brother or sister be naked, and destitute of daily food,

[16] And one of you say unto them, Depart in peace, be ye warmed and filled; notwithstanding ye give them not those things which are needful to the body; what doth it profit?

[17] Even so faith, if it hath not works, is dead, being alone.

God owns it All, which means He owns "*us*." He created all things – He is our Creator. He created <u>us</u> for His purpose and Glory. Believe it, as we go through our daily routines, and as we get up (by HIS Grace) every morning, as the alarm sounds, we breathe life (air flows through our lungs). *IT IS HIM WHO PROVIDES.* [1]Our bodies would be useless, to any alarm regardless of "how loud," it would not matter, if the breath of life were not in us. "He," God gives us these gifts daily, and we MUST realize that the gift of living or waking up daily is a daily gift from the creator.

[1] God provides us life so that we rise daily.

[2] **God** provides the strength so that we are capable of getting up each day and performing.

[3] He provides the strength to make the living that we earn, regardless of how much or how little.

> [4] As for our minds, and the ability to create, think, develop, and function daily, ALL are given through the Father because of His love for us.

Therefore, the money that we EARN does belong to HIM. HE FORMED THE MASTERPIECE; HE CREATED US AND ALL THE TALENTS THAT WE POSSESS; THE WISDOM, THE SKILLS, and ***All OPPORTUNTIES***. Yes, it all comes from the Creator of Heaven and Earth. The **Creator of all living things creates each opportunity that leads to each level of success. And yes, opportunities** are given through the development of events that **He puts into motion**.

God has provided a guideline of how He desires that we receive or use the talents that we have, the attitudes that we should have, and how we should feel about stewarding *HIS Money*. The guidelines of money and *stewardship are outlined in HIS Word*. Let us take a look at the many ways we should look at the talents and gifts that He has given us.

REMEMBER THAT ALL BELONGS TO GOD AND ALL IS PROVIDED THROUGH HIM.

Psalm 24:1, (KJV)

> [1]The earth is the LORD's, and the fullness thereof; the world, and they that dwell therein.

None of us earned life, BUT IT WAS GIVEN TO US. It's all a gift from God. All of creation is a gift of God.

None of us can earn that, and if we think we have earned it, we have made a mistake. We underestimate what God has given us, the world itself, and all the blessings that are on the earth; God gave that to us. It does not matter what you invented, or what you created, God's hand was ON IT. He orchestrates the plan, creates the man, and implements the plan.

God gave life and IMPLANTED the plan IN US, and STEP BY STEP, FED US THE PLAN, GROWING AND PERFECTING US INTO THE CREATION THAT WOULD FINALLY IMPLEMENT THE PLAN THAT WOULD HELP OTHERS, AND WIN SOULS FOR HIS GLORY. WE did not earn it, but we were the *Vessels*. He chose us to gift and change the lives of many with the talents/gifts that He instilled in us. Our abilities and everything we have are gifts from the creator of all things.

Sovereign and Grace – Inherent

When we think about it, the fact that God owns everything makes perfect sense. God created us, and the earth that we inhabit. We had no inherent right to exist outside of Him. The sovereignty of God is why we exist. Through God's sovereign and grace we are given life and the world that surrounds us. The majestic God has lovingly provided and given His children great promises, and we are here due to His desire to have a relationship with us, and the great love He has for us.

As Daniel references:

Daniel 4:17, (NS)

> **17The decision is announced by messengers, the holy ones declare the verdict, so that the living may know that the Most High is sovereign over all kingdoms on earth and gives them to anyone he wishes and sets over them the lowliest of people.**

Daniel 4:17, (KJV)

> **17 This matter is by the decree of the watchers, and the demand by the word of the holy ones: to the intent that the living may know that the most High ruleth in the kingdom of men, and giveth it to whomsoever he will, and setteth up over it the basest of men.**

Daniel 5:17, (KJV)

> [17] Then Daniel answered and said before the king, Let thy gifts be to thyself, and give thy rewards to another; yet I will read the writing unto the king, and make known to him the interpretation.

An important principle to keep firmly in mind is to understand whose money we are talking about. It is not our money, and if we are married, it is not our mate's money. It is God's money. Yet, because a marriage is a union, all monies are united as well, but God owns it.

God's ownership is a foreign concept to most of us. We like to think of *our* money and *our* possessions as if we are the owners. Yet the Bible makes it clear that God owns everything.

Deuteronomy 10:14, (KJV)

> [14] Behold, the heaven and the heaven of heavens is the LORD's thy God, the earth also, with all that therein is.

(Haggai 2:8, KJV)

> *"The silver is mine and the gold is mine," saith the God of Host.*

You might ask, "But don't some Bible verses, such as Proverbs 3:9 and Colossians 4:15, refer to people owning possessions?" Yes, they do, but underlying in these verses is the knowledge that everything belongs to God.

In 1 Chronicles 29:11, there is another scripture that states God owns everything, and He should be exalted because He is head over all.

Yes, all receive, as God works to develop and show each of His children the light of the world as stewards, teachers, or counselors. We bring the gift of God to the forsaken. We open the door of the love that God desires, and that we bestow on others, and as a result, we bring them closer to HIM (God). It is the love, the invitation that scoops them up, and the Word comes forward and wins their hearts to worship Him as their maker.

God allows mankind to be stewards over HIS money; the role of stewardship should be served and given freely, and faithfully. God summons His servants to serve and honor the needs of the poor.

GOD SINCERELY LOOKS AT HOW AND WHAT WE SPEND MONEY ON. IN REALITY, we are **all** His STEWARDS. THE people that are privileged financially are chosen by God to steward sums of money or possessions to people (it is a gift to be financially privileged). Stewardship is God's way of *completing the task of establishing success of needed money* to individuals/organizations in need.

AS RESOURCE TO H**ELP THE POOR AND INDIVIDUALS IN NEED, GOD WORKS THROUGH MAN**.

Yes, He works through man to feed His sheep His Word and to distribute His money. Heaven is the LORD's, thy God, and the earth with all its wonders. All should see the works and love of God. The gifts of compassion, giving, wisdom, and financial growth, all demonstrates God's love.

Therefore, should we give and provide to Christians and Non-Christians? Yes, Yes, and Yes, It is a demonstration of God's love. It opens our eyes to the sovereign of God. God's love demonstrates His grace, despite our sins. Let us focus on several scriptures that support the above notes:

Deuteronomy 15:7, (KJV)

> [7] If there is a poor man among your brothers in any of the towns of the land that the LORD your God is giving you, do not be hardhearted or tightfisted toward your poor brother.

Deuteronomy 15:11, (KJV)

> [11] There will always be poor people in the land. Therefore I command you to be openhanded toward your brothers and toward **the poor** and needy in your land.

CHAPTER 4

BLESSED AND PRIVILEGED

Are you one that can proudly say you are privileged and have a large home, and possibly two or three properties? Do you drive an elite auto? Do you have the privilege of having money to travel, or can go out to a nice restaurant and eat such items as filet mignon, caviar, or prime ribs often, more than once a week? If you are privileged, which means ALL of your family needs are financially met, with an ongoing excess; you can afford to travel often, to take trips out of the country, travel first class on a plane, or own your own private jet, then more than likely you have resources available to you which is extra income an excess or overflow of income.

If you are one that at times you find yourself alone because not many people that you find can live life on the same level as yourself. There are so many of your friends and associates that have limited access to money and cannot travel, entertain, or go out as frequently as you can. You seem to always have to pick up the bill and/or pay the tip. Being an entrepreneur allows you the freedom to travel and gives you a flexible, self-controllable work schedule. In your absence, you have staff that covers business matters for you. Perhaps you have notoriety, influence, and money, therefore, you are privileged or blessed.

Life should be full of giving, sharing, and investing in others. If you are a child of God, God has more than likely chosen you to take care of others financially, yes, choose to partake in giving to others and assuring that God's gift of wealth as you discern and help meet the needs of those who lack. To be blessed, to be the vessel, gifted to give is a privilege, providing the light to others. To shine and help others are part of God's purpose for your life.

Yes, sincerely God has blessed you. Do you ever wonder why God has provided you with the financial blessings? As you know, many people have talents and the ability to perform and earn a substantial income, but they use their talent in the church or just causally, without large earnings. You were given the blessing of financial success, God opened that door, He sent people to you, and He provided favor for your promotion. As you note, not many have the advantage of truly living leisurely, enjoying the many extras of life (theater, travel, workout clubs, Sport Games, Butlers, maids, private jet etc.....).

God has privileged you the gift of prosperity. Yes, prosperity, WHY? He has expectations, as He overly and abundantly gives to the privileged for a purpose. If you are a person that receives as noted in the sentences above, as God has given He desires that financial successful people give back in return. God provides the Gift of prosperity that befalls on those who have the compassion and discerning ability to give and love others, assisting others as the need arises. God provides gifts to each of us. Yes, the gift of giving financial support, God bestows on delegated Christians. God desires that no one has to go without food, clothes or shelter. As He placed each of us on this earth, He also made a provision to ensure that each is fed, taken care of. Take a look at the scripture that follows:

Matthew 6:26–34, (KJV) Notes:

> 26 Behold the fowls of the air: for they sow not, neither do they reap, nor gather into barns; yet your heavenly Father feedeth them. Are ye not much better than they?
>
> 27 Which of you by taking thought can add one cubit unto his stature?
>
> 28 And why take ye thought for raiment? Consider the lilies of the field, how they grow; they toil not, neither do they spin:
>
> 29 And yet I say unto you, That even Solomon in all his glory was not arrayed like one of these.

30 Wherefore, if God so clothe the grass of the field, which to day is, and to morrow is cast into the oven, shall he not much more clothe you, O ye of little faith?

31 Therefore take no thought, saying, What shall we eat? Or, What shall we drink? or, Wherewithal shall we be clothed?

32 (For after all these things do the Gentiles seek:) for your heavenly Father knoweth that ye have need of all these things.

33 But seek ye first the kingdom of God, and his righteousness; and all these things shall be added unto you.

34 Take therefore no thought for the morrow: for the morrow shall take thought for the things of itself. Sufficient unto the day is the evil thereof.

What about those born with wealth that are privileged?

The wealthy and the privileged are challenged; many are required to discern who and what to spend money on. The skills of stewardship are challenging. Money can be the root of evil, however; fighting the temptation to spend and lavish oneself with worldly goods can be a challenge. To live by the Word of God and make the right choices will allow the Holy Spirit to lead the way.

Therefore, to choose the best options to meet the needs of self as the steward of God's money can be work. Yes, as a privileged receiver of prosperity, you are required to give as you discern the need to give. Believe it, you are called to give and discern the needs of others. The Holy Spirit, tugs on your heart, aids in the decision to help those with a sincere need. Giving should not be withheld (family, friends, fellow man, as all are your neighbors). Caution should be taken, not to judge if the individual is Godly or UnGodly, but to give to all, to the saved and unsaved. Giving extends the recognition of God's love for all.

Galatians 5:14, (NIV)

[14] The entire law is summed up in a single command: "Love your neighbor as yourself."

YOUR NEIGHBOR, AS STATED IN THE SCRIPTURE ABOVE, YOU SHOULD SEE YOUSELF! IF YOU PROVIDE FOR YOURSELF IN THE SAME CIRCUMSTANCES, YOU SHOULD PROVIDE TO YOUR NEIGHBOR AS YOU ARE CALLED TO DO; AS A PRIVILEGED VESSEL, GOD GIVES IN ABUNDANCE TO YOU SO THAT YOU MAY ASSIST OTHERS IN NEED.

Why store up treasures on earth? Are you seeking to take possessions with you, or leave your possessions on earth? Materialistic items serve no purpose. The scripture advises man on just how to view the collection of earthly possessions in Matthew 6:19-21.

Matthew 6:19-21, (KJV)

[19] Lay not up for yourselves treasures upon earth, where moth and rust doth corrupt, and where thieves break through and steal:

[20] But lay up for yourselves treasures in heaven, where neither moth nor rust doth corrupt, and where thieves do not break through nor steal:

[21] For where your treasure is, there will your heart be also.

As the scripture states, we must guard our hearts against embracing and cherishing earthly possessions. As records show, we are never content with the level of income that we earn. As we increase our income levels, our desire to increase the quality of items changes, and the money, regardless of how much, is never enough. The typical individual never reaches a satisfactory income level. Enough is never enough. Every increase demands a new increase, and it becomes never ending. Believe!

Look at the poor in a new perspective, give to organizations, to ones that are not privileged and need a financial vessel. Step in to help as needed, be a giver. If you know of someone in need of prayer it is okay to extend prayer for them. But do not hold back financially, take the initiative to help by giving, give what you can, for God has provided enough.

In reality, in praying you ask God for a source to help, yet you can play a part by helping, as the source!

If you see a need, act on that need. Justification should not be required. An explanation of how or why an individual fell to the level of having the need is not ours to question. We must act knowing that they are in the position or in the condition of need, because God has allowed it and has now placed the awareness of their need on us, so that we will discern the validity of that need and respond to the need. God has a plan and a desire to place on our hearts to help. God has not forsaken them, but created the way or the source, with the full knowledge that He will summon divine encounters, as to see if we, as His servants, will honor the needs of the poor.

REMEMBER IT ALL BELONGS TO HIM. God is at work! The wealthy, the middle class, and the poor are interconnected, a three-fold connection. Therefore we can stand strong together. As Christians, will we walk and provide; standing on the Word, standing in the gap, blessing the poor as needed?

In God's Word, God repeatedly encourages everyone to help their brother. God knows what we can do, and all should take care of the ones in need. God also commands that we give from our flow of blessings, and it will surely be returned to us in abundant. In fact, God has GIFTED many to take on financial roles, and with the expectation to give to His people, organizations of ministries, businesses, churches or individuals seeking help; each should stand and fulfill the need. Please, never forget that through God's blessings, the holders of wealth are given through the grace that God placed on our life. We are the recipients, the stewards of God's possessions, Yes, "God's Money."

All who receive in abundance are provided an opportunity, an open door by God, to give and provide freely. God gives to each of us gifts that we use to earn a living. God provides the air we breathe, the ability to walk, talk, sing, dance, discern, write, or possess any talent. The skills and abilities that we possess come from God. Every opportunity that has opened for us to succeed, God has opened. Yes, He awards the opportunities. ALL IS HIS. We can downplay any of the statements in His Word, but believe it, YOU BELONG TO HIM! You Are His and ALL that you achieve, God placed favor on the efforts and the abilities of each advancement. It is His favor or grace on your life that allows your success to manifest. In fact, you could not advance without His hands on it! Each level of advancement is due to Him placing His hands on the goal and allowing the advancement to manifest. IT HAS NEVER BEEN YOU! BELIEVE IT! ALL THAT YOU HAVE ACHIEVED IS GOD'S WORK! GOD WORKS THROUGH MAN, AND IT IS ACCORDING TO HIS GRACE and HIS PLAN.

YET, You might think, or say, "I earned my money. No one gave me anything. I had to work hard for it." But GOD! Remember God in All Things.

It may be true that you put in long hours to get where you are. Yet it is God who created you and gave you the strength and talent to earn the money. God gave you the mind and the sharpness to think, produce, and excel in whatever area of success. He opened the door to the job or business and gave you favor. The best applicant does not always get the job or the business, for it is God's favor that wins the position/job/client. Yes, let's not downplay your win. Your success is God's favor.

Deuteronomy 8:17-18, (KJV)

> 17 And thou say in thine heart, My power and the might of mine hand hath gotten me this wealth.
>
> 18 But thou shalt remember the LORD thy God: for it is he that giveth thee power to get wealth that he may establish his covenant which he sware unto thy fathers, as it is this day.

1 Corinthians 4:7, (KJV)

> 7 For who maketh thee to differ from another? and what hast thou that thou didst not receive? now if thou didst receive it, why dost thou glory, as if thou hadst not received it?

To paraphrase, in the Bible, as I break down the words, one that boast about their achievements; for it says that one did nothing on its own accord; it all comes from a source provided by God or through God directly. Bottom line, God intervenes in all circumstances. Nothing occurs without Him knowing or allowing. Believe it!

Chapter 5

Entitlement

So, what are you entitled to? As you train for ten to twelve years or more, and complete the degree, practice day and night to master a given talent, honestly we are not entitled. The fact that God has made and provided us the ability, it all belongs to God; all of the money and the talent are given by God. All belongs to God! God takes care of us and all of our needs, He provides the things that sustain us, God does. You were made for the purpose of which God designed, and you exist to meet that purpose. Your financial status is actually fully owned by God. As an individual, we must remember to control our mind and our perception; not only how we view our earnings, but the money that governs the world around us. Federal, state, county, all government agencies and the money that exists is God's. Yes, it is.

In my spirit I desire to cover the need for individuals to look at money, people, God, and the distribution of God's money in a new perspective. God's blessings are available to all. We must remember that we all go through trials, which could mean periods of no to low income. Trials are only periods of times when we are tested, but anyone can receive the blessings of God financially. God has a plan for each child, and He knows who He will prosper, for God has predestined each one of us, and has a plan laid out. For what God has for you is set, and He will lead according to His plan. So we ask why are many of God's children financially crippled, leaning on society and the help of the wealthy to cover the basic necessities of life. God, in his plan, develops, teaches, and establishes the Christian, which glorifies God. The distribution of money is used as a teacher. The lack of income is also used to teach and to humble; it brings an understanding of Godly love according to God's will.

So are we entitled to anything, money, fame, prosperity? Seriously, it does not matter how hard we have worked, there is No Entitlement. We were created and are entitled to nothing. It seems harsh, however, the truth stands. God owns us, and everything that we achieve. God orchestrated the creation of all things, we belong to Him. Our education, our physical capabilities, our mind, and the ability to create, belongs to God. We are not entitled to the earnings, but God allows us to hold it! We are a steward of the money that is placed in our hands, but GOD'S POWER MANIFESTS THE EARNINGS. We Are Not entitled, in the sense that it belongs to us. God owns us and we are (His) stewards!

Surely, are you entitled to your earnings as we know that you put in the hours of study and/or practices to earn the mid-to-top dollars that you receive? We achieved in such areas of tennis, golf, or football, setting goals and achieving them. Maybe we attended school and earned a Ph.D., degree. Yes, maybe you gave up the man or the lady who stole your heart, or maybe we spent so much time in a book or practicing, that we did not explore a personal relationship, and several "Potential Mates got away!" Yet you completed your endeavors and became successful, with a substantial income, however, according to scripture the earnings are not yours.

God provides us the gift, the ability, the shelter, the transportation;, and the where-withal to master our goalsio. He placed in us the spirit to complete His vision for our lives. We are the work of the supreme God, the Father of all creation; all that consumes us belongs to Him, from the crown of our head to the bottom of our feet.

Many may oppose that statement and feel; I deserve this substantial income. I worked hard, my sister did not believe in me; my family was too busy to spend any time helping me achieve the dreams that I aspired. Mom and dad could not afford to do anything for me financially, but since they are my parents, I will acknowledge and give them their due respect. I have achieved and won, due to my personal sweat and perseverance. No one helped me to get here –Or– even if we feel we have one or two people who stuck by us, yet, only you accomplished the task! Now the substantial earnings belong to you!

The fact that we have ripped and sowed, finally obtaining a level of notoriety, it is ours to enjoy, spending it on the different pleasures in life! All the money and fame belongs to US ... yes? NO, God Owns, the least amount of money and the greatest wealth established by a man, IT IS GOD'S.

So, what is wrong with thinking that it is yours? GOD is not **Glorified.** God is lost in the midst! It is missing the love and submission of the beauty of God that He created in us and through us!

Did we not achieve through our own sweat? Was it not our effort and endurance that manifested the achievements? Yes, Yes, and Yes. However, look at entitlement in this way; God provided us life. God provided our strength. God provide us each day. God provided our mind, and He provided us the talent/gift/skill to excel. God provided us with health and determination. He opened the door, and gave us favor. God's favor allowed each promotion. His hands kept us standing, and it was God's hands that provided the breath of life, as life is not promised.

How many individuals do we know who have talents, but those talents have never manifested into anything spectacular? How many individuals has God used in other ways, who possibly had disabilities, and who could not achieve as you have achieved? God has a plan for every child's life. If you can follow the plan and live accordingly, success is ours. Yes, we participated and accomplished, as the Father's plan is implemented and the reward issued. God blessed as we completed the work that He placed in our path to complete. We are winners, because He chose us, the vessel that He favored or blessed.

It is His Blessing and His Celebration (For God receives the Glory!).

Therefore, in knowing that God provides, despite the challenges or the battles in life, it is good to know that He is with us during our journey. God increases and all of our success should be attributed to His work. Jehovah is the rewarder, our success should humble us to abide in and contribute to continuing the plan He has on our life.

The funds, as He has provisioned 10% to always be given as a tithe. The money that is awarded in addition to our tithe may be offered as a contribution, given to other sources. He has developed the resources. **God has made provisions and as the end times are in our midst, it is so important that we are aware that wealth/the overflow of income should be used to establish God's**

plan to assist the poor, which is God's desire that you distribute, and not store up material items on earth. All are stewards; therefore as vessels all should give in one way or another.

Chapter 6

Stewardship - When and How

Calling to Help the Poor

Although your role is to act as a steward, your position does not always mean that you provide actual monetary help. It might mean that you assist by providing labor, informational resources to help resolve issues, or paying such things as utilities, mortgage, or even providing groceries. Let us reflect on:

Proverbs 21:13, KJV

> 13"***Whoever shuts their ears to the cry of the poor will also cry out and not be answered",***

As we see the needs of others; we should attempt to fill that need.

GOD SINCERELY LOOKS AT HOW AND WHAT THE financially privileged spend. In reality, the wealthy are stewards of God's money. The financially secured should redistribute God's MONEY TO INDIVIDUALS/ORGANIZATIONS IN NEED. God's plan IS TO HELP THE POOR AND THOSE IN NEED, and as previously discussed, GOD WORKS THROUGH MAN. He works through man to feed His sheep the Word, to distribute financial support, and freely provide for people in need. Please understand that we all must give with no motives for payback, or we may provide a service/a deed, an action, which are all ways to give. Give with no expectation of receiving back. God will provide the return, as He freely gives; and in return we should give freely.

Take a look at: 1 John 3:17-18, (KJV)

> [17] But whoso hath this world's good, and seeth his brother have need, and shutteth up his bowels of compassion from him, how dwelleth the love of God in him?
>
> [18] My little children, let us not love in word, neither in tongue; but in deed and in truth.

King James Version (KJV)

Yes, ALL truly belongs to God. As we dig deeper into the Word, we come to a consensus of God's purpose:

In Colossians 16, the Bible references that all belongs to the creator. Yes, everything. So we can see in the scriptures noted that all, in reality, BELONGS to Him. And yet some would argue the point, "that I paid dramatic dues for my achievements. I SACRIFICED! How can it all belong to God? As mentioned in earlier chapters, He has given you the mental ability and skills to learn and perform. Can we honestly take the credit for physically getting up each day, or having the ability to create?

Can we take the credit for developing ideas that excel, or winning a race with exceptional speed? Who provides the skill, the ability—who GIVES ALL TALENTS TO ALL PEOPLE AND PROVIDES THE SOURCES, THE MONEY, AND THE VICTORY OVER THE COMPETITOR? THE ANWSER IS GOD! REMEMBER, it is God's Provision!

Give to All

Therefore, that leads to the questions, should we give regardless whether that individual is spiritually, filled or seeking God? Should we give and provide to Christians and Non-Christians? Yes, Yes, and triple, Yes! It is a demonstration of the love of God and opens our eyes to the sovereign of God. God loves everyone; all falls short, all are still yet sinners!

Romans 3:10-12, and 23 (KJV)

[10] As it is written, There is none righteous, no, not one:

[11] There is none that understandeth, there is none that seeketh after God.

[12] They are all gone out of the way, they are together become unprofitable; there is none that doeth good, no, not one.

[23] *For everyone has sinned; we all fall short of God's glorious standard.* The price (or consequence) of sin is death.

Stewardship – Gifts

When successful individuals can accept the realization that despite the core talents they feel are natural, and that are given BY GOD, EACH GIFT IS ISSUED OR CAN BE TAKEN AWAY. Monies earned, due to our gifts belongs to the Father. We should use to focus on the needs of others, and redistribute to others. ***God has chosen vessels to give as they possess the gift of prosperity.***

Many have gifts, but some do not aspire or use them to gain wealth. God sometimes desires that special/given gifts are used on a different level. Many strive to reach a level of financial success, but only by the "Grace of God" will it be accomplished.

Look at your success and earnings as a role in STEWARDSHIP. GOD HAS GRANTED YOU THE OPPORTUNITY AND THE HONOR TO BE A STEWARD FOR HIM! ***It is sincerely an Honor.***

Stewardship also falls under the heading of tithing, giving as the bible commands 10%. Yet physically taking the initial to give when you know and can see there is a need, is a gift of discernment; having the ability to discern the need of others. It does not have to be an announcement or a fund raiser, but God gives us the ability to discern the needs of each individual. In many cases we can see individuals who are hurting financially. It is visible in their expressions, transportation, or physical appearances at times. Stewardship should be provided as we take on the role to help.

True stewardship is one of the gifts that God gives, and He expects us to honor as he provides excess for that purpose.

Stewardship – Tithing

Tithing gives us the opportunity to follow or obey what God has asked of us. That is to tithe one-tenth of His money back to His Church to assist with growth, Pastoring, Evangelism, yes, the financial burdens of maintaining the property, staff, and leadership He has put into place to manifest His plans teaching and helping to feed His sheep (which includes, The Word, The bible).

As previously discussed in, **1 John 3:17-18, to see your brother in need and choose not to help, in some way, then the love of God does not abide in you.**

We can choose to offer prayer to those that need, but if we have resources, and send the one in need away not fulfilling their need(s); God knows, because He knows our resources and skills, precisely what we have to offer or give.

Matthew 19:24, (KJV)

> 24 And again I say unto you, it is easier for a camel to go through the eye of a needle, than for a rich man to enter into the kingdom of God.

God`s Word definitely indicates that sincerely giving is what He expects everyone to do. Giving with a pure heart glorifies the Father. Please note the verses below; as sleep falls on each man, God desires that our attitudes and hearts reflect in Matthew 6:19-21.

Matthew 6: 19-21, (KJV)

> 19 Lay not up for yourselves treasures upon earth, where moth and rust doth corrupt, and where thieves break through and steal:

> 20 But lay up for yourselves treasures in heaven, where neither moth nor rust doth corrupt, and where thieves do not break through nor steal:

21 For where your treasure is, there will your heart be also.

Again, our way of thinking about money should line up with God's way; it is a better way, for it is the perspective of love and giving. The job of keeping up with riches or money matters may consume an individual of wealth. We must let go, give, and know all earthly possessions are Gods. We must learn to release and give freely. Follow God's example and give freely.

We may develop attitudes, and it can get into our hearts, but we need to replace it with the truth of God's Word. God owns it, and we must believe and live accordingly.

We should ask ourselves –

Why should the money we earn be handed to a stranger who we know nothing about? How do we discern who to give to? Do we change our lifestyle to accommodate others? Perhaps, we may have to change some policies in our country that cause so many to be poor, while few become rich. We should have concerns about seeking to make changes. Yet, how or where should we start? Change starts with wisdom, in which God provides.

The wisdom of God, It is like a two-edged sword that goes deeply into our being and challenges us, and the Word of God. The wisdom of God will help in discerning who and when to provide blessings into the lives of others. Prayer wisdom and discernment are gifts to aid in helping the poor. The Holy Spirit and the searching of our hearts, should lead us in all decisions.

As Jesus looked on, he professed in scripture a prime example of giving, as one who freely gives in reading Luke 21:1-4.

Luke 21:1-4, (KJV)

1Jesus looked up and saw the rich putting their gifts into the offering box,

2And he saw a poor widow put in two small copper coins.

3And he said, "Truly, I tell you, this poor widow has put in more than all of them.

> [4]For they all contributed out of their abundance, but she out of her poverty put in all she had to live on.

Not everyone is called to give their all or their last to tithe or give to others, nor should they. However, we all should be willing to sacrifice at times to give to the needs of the community, the church, or our fellow man. Freely give with thanksgiving that God has provided enough that we may share. To be the Chosen Vessel, to give is what God has gifted some to do, and others to contribute to out of love. Loving our neighbors as ourselves, would allow us the opportunity to implement this act of love to others.

Proverbs 11:24, (KJV)

> [24] There is that scattereth, and yet increaseth; and there is that withholdeth more than is meet, but it tendeth to poverty.

The scripture references that some will give freely and see increases in their lives, while others withhold and see decreases, despite the fact they did not take from the extra (plenty) that God provided them.

In Matthew 10:8, (KJV), the scripture promotes to give freely.

> [8] Heal the sick, cleanse the lepers, raise the dead, cast out devils: freely ye have received, freely give.

The scriptures above profess to give “Freely”.

Chapter 7

Beggar Man — Thief

Attitude

God`s Word definitely indicates that sincere giving is what He expects everyone to do. In reality, freely giving demonstrates God`s love for mankind. Giving with a pure heart glorifies God.

To reach high levels of financial success is a gift, "For much is given; much is expected," God has a plan to manifest individuals in His time and in multiple ways. However, during the process, as stewards, we should supply financial support to the needy. To give should be natural, to assist those who show evidence of needing material items such as food, clothes, and shoes. Items for maintenance of hair, skin, teeth, and medical could also be supplied. If we can reach out and provide a connection that helps to service them at no cost or low cost, then we will enable the families to live and stay afloat.

GIVE!

Volunteering or offering a service at no cost is one way of giving. An individual who is self-employed, or an entrepreneur, can give by offering a needed service for free, on a special day or for a special event, on a monthly or an annual basis. You are the boss; the decision maker. As a promotion, give to those in need, and it will increase your business. Become a Vessel to those who cannot afford your service (or do not qualify). GIVING AWAY A DAY OF SERVICE CAN AND/OR WILL INCREASE YOUR BUSINESS. IT IS ALSO A TAX WRITE-OFF. Word of mouth for a service well done spreads, and appreciation proclaimed from the mouth of the receiver promotes new business.

We believe that the things that we have are ours. This attitude gets into our hearts, causing us to become slaves to money. The Truth: God owns everything. A negative or selfish attitude about money can in turn, become the sinful act of greed. Greed is not of God.

As noted in recent data, as much as 1% in society has exceptional wealth, and about 99% struggle. Success is God's blessing on our lives.

NEGATIVE ATITUDES, NEGATIVE RESPONSES AND STIPULATIONS, COME FROM THE INFLUENCE OF THE ENEMY. IF LOVE COMES FROM GOD THEN ACTIONS OR THOUGHTS THAT DO NOT REFLECT LOVE OF OUR NEIGHBOR, ARE ***NOT OF GOD***.

Many people have a preconception that receiving benefits from government sources such as food stamps, Temporary Assistance for Needy Families "TANF", and SSI – Supplemental Security Income (or Social Security) checks, are means of living off of working individuals or the government. They feel that a lot of people that receive benefits are using the system/government, but in reality, God gives all, provides all, and approves all. Many are in transition, as God has a plan, and it is not for our judgment. He has allowed hindrance financially to as to promote an experience new awareness and growth. He will open new doors as His plan permits. God promotes and demotes. He let me know, as I started on one of the programs, not to be concerned, but receive ALL, It belongs to Him.

Are Social Service recipients beggars? God's favor goes out on different levels and He uses man to represent His mercy and grace. God sometimes places us in positions of need so that He may teach others how to give, showing the act of compassion and love. As well, God uses this level of income sometimes as a teacher, to teach us how to be humble. In creating a world of multiple levels of financial statuses, He can demonstrate blessings and change the hearts of man. If everyone had wealth, the need for compassion would not exist and greed and selfishness would only increase. Compassion, love and selflessness comes out of the lack of money, as does the understanding and the need for God. God desires that we stay close to Him, and having a relationship with Him, praying and building faith, are in essence, God's desires in all situations.

Consider the attitudes of man, and the fact that selfishness and greed would cancel out love and thankfulness, and even the slightest desire to give would not exist. Many would never seek God. The world would sincerely be so heartless that men would not have bonding relationships. Meaningful families who work in harmony would be hard to find. It is a fact that the more a wealthy man receives, the more he wants. Therefore, there would not be enough money for the wealthy, and many would desire more by taking/stealing from one another.

This **equates to greed**. Love would be contingent on money, or how much money one has. A loveless world would exist. That is not the plan of God, for God is love. The sole reason for creating man would be forsaken. Love, relationships, and teaching love, as the first commandment, would also be forsaken. An emphasis to love God and to love one's neighbor as one loves oneself, is the plan of God.

(Mark 12; 29-31). The essence of the first two commandments, to love God and to love thy neighbor, should be every man's priority. It must manifest!

God has a plan and it is not for our judgment. As people abide, support, and learn to take a position of love, helping should be the attitude towards anyone going through a financial season of hardship.

Do not Hate: Social Attitudes – Department of Social Services

As I write, I desire to bring to the forefront the negative connotations that go along with receiving EBT, the food card associated with the Department of Social Services. In shopping, cashiers, and other store employees questioned if you are justly receiving the benefit. How can you look and assume the need or judge one's needs? Yes, you can approximate, but surely you cannot define. If by looking, nothing is obvious in the appearance; many store employees get an attitude. Of course, many feel that you have falsified papers to receive these benefits, and their complete attitude towards you changes. It is unbelievable. As you shop in high income areas, maybe you had an appointment in an area and stop to make a purchase. Many in-store clerks have a problem with a shopper that use such a card (EBT) and may casually pick you by asking questions. It is not the norm in that area, but yet you should not have to answer questions, on how many children you have or if you have foster children.

We must remember God gives and works it all. If anyone has been approved to receive, it is certain that God has provided favor. God has placed His hand on it and has provided that source for that season of life. He challenges us to experience hardship so that we can learn to be a blessing to others (in some cases). Yet, hardship may be experience for many reasons. God provides a journey of instructions to move us from one level to the next. God carries us through new experiences and challenges, sometimes cutting down to the raw of our being before bringing us out and cleaning us up.

Whether or not we receive a promotion is based on our understanding of the experience. Society should not judge. God will close the door when the time is right. No one should try to determine who or why someone is on social assistance. As a believer or supporter, always look to help so that the challenge of learning and growing can be completed. God has a purpose; poverty is usually only a temporary state. In faith, many will experience low income, but will eventually come out and experience a higher level of God. Yes, God's love will manifest itself in the hearts of the poor, and the opportunity to serve someone during a season of hardship should give us honor as God's work is completed.

We should erase the thoughts that people on such programs are beggars, sluggers or thieves. God uses individuals to teach others, as well as to establish love on earth. Be a teacher, show love and embrace the opportunity to do what you can!

In reality, are individuals on such programs beggars or thieves?

***Qualifying for services that are in reality a program that God has outlined to assist the poor, has many challenges. One of the challenges is the government's stipulation that all food purchases must be cold food. It bewilders me as to why this stipulation has been put into place. Items that are precooked and served hot in the grocery store cannot be purchased with the food card, EBT. If you are eligible for food and you are homeless, you cannot purchase a hot meal from the deli. I do not know all the technicalities as to why, but the homeless, or any individual or family who lives in a small room, motel/hotel, without a kitchen or a kitchenette, would really appreciate a cooked meal versus cold cuts/raw meat or canned goods. The need to have electricity available too, is also a factor that is a disadvantage, for a low or no income individual. Many live without electric and cannot cook a meal. Needless it is a rough call to say 'no' to food in the grocery store that may not be purchased due to it being prepared and hot. Seriously, that is exact what many that use the card needs. Why are they denied?

At times, pots and pans may be a problem, as these instruments are needed to prepare a cooked meal. If the benefit is allowed, what difference does it make if the food is hot and ready to eat? To stipulate that hot items cannot be purchased should be changed. That is a battle that should be addressed. How do we change such stipulations and/or restrictions?

Please believe me; it is difficult to get approved and to stay on the program. The government has placed their hands in it and desires to master who is awarded benefits, based on a strict criteria. To prove the need is really a challenge. I personally have been subjected to the system and spoke to so many others who have experienced a constant challenge to receive assistant. Anyone who has been through the experience knows that there are new pre-qualifications periodically.

The recipient on the program is always questioned, and though there is no way the caseworker will allow anyone to receive benefits for a lengthy period of time without constantly monitoring their income, the caseworker always reviews the criteria, challenging previous information provided, and questioning every letter, check stub, every change to ensure that qualifications are met in order to continue receiving the benefit or to stay on the program.

The process is detailed, and it appears that the recipients are guilty of falsely receiving benefits, and have to prove monthly that they are not ripping the government off. They have to prove weekly that they are seeking employment. If they receive TANF benefits, a list of all job searches must be given. In most states they must show up to a job workshop to provide a job search list.

If the recipients find part-time employment, that job can actually work against them, and benefits can be stopped if they find temporary work. Yes, part-time work can work against you (you make enough to cancel out the benefit, but not enough to cover your household expenses). Benefits may be stopped, and starting over can take 45 days or more while trying to find a solution to income dilemmas. Sincerely, finding full-time work or a full-time income source, permanently is the best solution. Considering all, for the one that need the benefit of social services is truly a blessing from God. It is an unhappy place to be on a financial level of low or no income, but it is God's call, a faith call. God provides all!

To own an auto or a house goes against one who at some point may have been a progressive citizen, and for some reason lost a position or may be going through a financial struggle. A mother with children who owns an auto is at a disadvantage. In reality, to have assets of any type counts against you, regardless if you acquired them before the hardship (living in a house you own, can work against you). So to receive is not a joy, it is a temporary solution that can enable you in many ways. It is a faith call.

The process insults those who are truly in need and desire to transition from assistance to self-sufficiency. Most of the caseworkers seek ways to reduce their load and disqualify the benefit without seeking a solution (this is due to over loading and over working the caseworkers). Their attitudes are government focused. Their desire is to move the paper processing off of their desk, even if it causes the individual applying additional hardships. Therefore, please believe me, most are receiving benefits only because they need them until things change. As the individual seeks assistance, they are made to feel they are inadequate or just seeking a handout. To those who do not understand, it is challenging.

No one should judge, God has full control. Yes, God allows the approval. God places favor on the mind of the representative to approve government benefits (there is always a source that can go against you and you can be disapproved). As I mentioned before, to own property, a house or car, can cause disqualification. GOD wins the battles and the approval is all His. I truly believe nothing happens by chance.

Are there truly people who are manipulating the government and receive benefits based on falsified information? What about people living on the streets, are they beggars? Truly they are going from one organization to the next, receiving food, sleeping under bridges, on the streets, or living off of the land. Can we say that these are God's people? Are they faithfully participating as a part of, "The Church" or Church Community?

Let`s review the facts. God is a provider of all things; all creation, all money, all land is His. He provides for all living creations. If God has provided for the birds, He has made a provision to provide for all living things. As for mankind, He has a provision to provide for all mankind through the gift of wealth that He bestowed on the selected Vessels of Prosperity, to redistribute His money as He sees fit, and in some cases He directly decrees that we give to a particular person or organization. God controls everything and will disqualify those who try to manipulate the system.

God does not allow misuse of the benefit or money. He brings awareness to those who misuse the system, and the benefits of those not in need are canceled. Yet the paper trails and demands of receiving benefits are difficult. God is the source used to get the individual to a stable and promotional level. At times, a period of preparation is needed. In other words, God gives us assistance while He prepares us.

As previously discussed, stewardship of God`s money is given to man. Those who are gifted financially should always seek to give to a needy cause. God has chosen, equipped, and prepared us for the purpose of giving. Preparation will consist of special talents given by God. The door is open to education fulfillment and completion, as well as the escalation and promotion in corporate society. These are all ways He uses man to create financial growth.

Proverbs 11:25, (NASB)

> **25 A generous person will be prosperous, And he who waters will himself be watered.**

Change your view, look at the poor in a new perspective. Seek to give to organizations. If you know of someone in need, pray and take the initiative to help by giving, for God has provided you. Look for ways to help, if you look you will find you have more than enough. If there is a need, act on that need. Justification is not needed. No explanation of how or why one is in the position or in the condition they are in, or why God has forsaken them is necessary. God has brought that individual to that level as to show His grace and mercy, and he has placed that person in your circle. Therefore, you are designated to be a source.

Summon others to fulfill the needs and create the way or the source with the full knowledge that He will summon a divine encounter as to see if we, as His serverants, will honor the needs of the poor. ALL BELONGS TO HIM. God is at work. He works on the wealthy, the middle class, and the poor by interconnecting and seeking to see if the Christian will walk and provide, standing on the Word and blessing the poor. God's Word repeatedly encourages all to take care of others in need. Give from the overflow of blessing and it will surely be returned to you one hundredfold.

All that is received in abundance is in reality, a reciprocal of God's Money. God owns you. He owns All Money, and He provides all opportunities and opens every door. God gives each of us gifts that we use to earn money. God provides the air that we breathe, the ability to walk, talk, sing, dance, discern, write, or have charisma abilities. ANY TALENT/SKILL that we possess comes from God. Every opportunity that has opened for us to succeed, God has opened and awarded the opportunity. YES, ALL IS HIS—ALL IS HIS—THAT INCLUDES YOU!

The realization is that the core talents that successful people feel are natural and are given BY GOD. EACH GIFT IS HIS TO PROMOTE OR TO TAKE AWAY. Everyone has gifts, but some do not aspire to use them to gain wealth. God may desire that the gifts are used on a different level. Modesty, or to be humble is, "adored" by the Father. Look at your success and earning as a role in STEWARDSHIP, THAT GOD HAS GRANTED YOU THE OPPORTUNITY AND THE HONOR TO BE A STEWARD FOR HIM!

Proverbs 19:17, (NASB)

> 17Whoever is generous to the poor lends to the Lord, and he will repay him for his deeds.

As I look in **<u>Matthew (5:42),</u> it basically says to give and do not refuse one in need.**

Change the way you view the poor. Look at it in a new perspective, and look at the money you receive in a different light. Give if God has provided you extra. The Word notes that you should tithe 10% and save 10% off the top of your earnings, and then pay bills and spend on the things you need. Afterward, you should take the initiative to help by giving, if you have extra at this point. God has provided to you, and you should plant a new seed.

If you see a need, act on that need. Justification or how or why the condition came about is not needed. God has brought that individual to that level as to show his grace and mercy. He has summoned others as well (you) to fulfill the needs and create the way or source. with the full knowledge that He will summon a divine encounter. Therefore, you should honor the needs of the poor.

God is at work, He works on the wealthy, the middle class, and the poor by interconnecting and seeking to see if the Christian will walk and provide as Standing on the Word, blessing the poor. In God's Word repeatedly, He encourages all to take care of those in need. Give from our overflow, providing a blessing, knowing that God will always provide.

All, in reality, are reciprocals of God's Money. God owns you, and He owns All Money. He provides all opportunities and opens every door. God gives each of us gifts that we use to earn money. God provides the air that we breathe, the ability to walk, to talk, to dance, to discern, or write. ANY TALENT/SKILL that we possess comes from God. Every opportunity that has opened for us to succeed, God has opened, and He awards that opportunity. YES, ALL IS HIS—YOUR Success is His success, and it all BELONGS TO HIM!

Luke 6:30-38, (KJV)

> [30] Give to every man that ask the of thee; and of him that taketh away thy goods ask them not again.
>
> [31] And as ye would that men should do to you, do ye also to them likewise.
>
> [32] For if ye love them which love you, what thank have ye? for sinners also love those that love them.
>
> [33] And if ye do good to them which do good to you, what thank have ye? for sinners also do even the same.
>
> [34] And if ye lend to them of whom ye hope to receive, what thank have ye? for sinners also lend to sinners, to receive as much again.
>
> [35] But love ye your enemies, and do good, and lend, hoping for nothing again; and your reward shall be great, and ye shall be the children of the Highest: for he is kind unto the unthankful and to the evil.
>
> [36] Be ye therefore merciful, as your Father also is merciful.

37 Judge not, and ye shall not be judged: condemn not, and ye shall not
be condemned: forgive, and ye shall be forgiven:

38 Give, and it shall be given unto you; good measure, pressed down,
and shaken together, and running over, shall men give into your
bosom. For with the same measure that ye mete withal it shall be
measured to you again.

God`s Word definitely indicates that sincere giving is what He expects everyone to do. In reality, it freely demonstrates His love for mankind. Giving with a pure heart glorifies the Father.

All SHOULD HONOR THE SOURCES THAT GOD HAS PLACED IN MAN TO BE STEWARDS FOR HIM! NOTE THE SCRIPTURES BELOW AS A REFERENCE:

1 John 3:17-18, (KJV)

17 But whoso hath this world's good, and seeth his brother have need,
and shutteth up his bowels of compassion from him, how dwelleth the
love of God in him?

18 My little children, let us not love in word, neither in tongue; but
indeed, and in truth.

Galatians 6:9-10, (KJV)

9 And let us not be weary in well doing: for in due season we shall reap,
if we faint not.

10 As we have therefore opportunity, let us do good unto all men,
especially unto them who are of the household of faith.

Look and think of the money you have and the distributions of the money in a new perspective. God blesses His children in many ways, some with a large financial success. God has a plan for each of His children, and knows who He will prosper. For whom God had predestined, He has a plan laid out. For what God has for you is set for you, and He will lead you according to His plans.

Then why are so many of God's children financially crippled, leaning on society and the help of the wealthy to cover the basic necessities of life? God, in his plans for developing and teaching, established growth and appreciation for the all Christians. The distribution of money is used as a teacher. Wealth is earned, and blessings are appreciated; however, the love and extending of love to us is taught.

How, who, and when do you help others by giving and sharing? God blesses through others, (Psalm 24:1). God distributes money according to inheritances and the blessings He desires in the life of that individual. God pre-destine, He knows the beginning and the end.

None of us earned life, it is a gift from God. All of creation is a gift from God. None of us can earn that. Therefore, if we think we've earned it, we are seriously mistaken. We underestimate what God has given us. The world itself and all the blessings that exist within the earth, God gave naturally. We did nothing to earn it, our individual lives are gifts. Our skills/abilities and every talent that we have are of God.

In the next chapter the Pope revealed in a letter some of the problems that he saw, as to open our eyes to many issues. Briefly there are paraphrased notes with limited concerns, as you read please note that not much has changed in 50 years.

Chapter 8

Summation of Pope Paul VI Letter –March 26, 1967

Outdated, Yet Relevant

In looking at the Pope's notes, I have completed a summation of the beliefs of the Pope who could foresee the need for change in joining together to help all people progress. I ask that you briefly read over the paraphrased notes as the concerns noted were written in 1965 and sadly, many of the problems still exist today (2016).

<u>As the Pope thoughts are outlined in the notes below:</u>

- ***The progressive development of people is of concern to the Church. This is true in the case of people who are trying to escape the ravages of hunger, poverty, endemic disease and ignorance; of those who are seeking a larger share in the benefits of civilization and improvement of human qualities.***
- ***The Church's duty is to help men explore the problem. The hungry nations of the world cry out to the people blessed with abundance. And the Church asks each and every man to hear his brother's plea, lovingly.***
- ***The disparity between rich and poor nations will increase rather than diminish; the rich nations are progressing with rapid strides while the poor nations move forward slowly.***

- ***The privileged minority enjoys the refinements of life, while the rest of the inhabitants, impoverished and disunited, "are deprived, and subsist in living and working conditions unworthy of the human person."***
- ***The Church seeks one goal: to carry forward the work of Christ. Christ gives witness to the truth; to save and to serve; not to judge.***
- ***We cannot disregard the welfare of those who will come after to increase human family.***
- ***Perspective rich and poor alike, can fall prey to materialism.***
- ***The material poverty of those who lack the bare necessities of life verses those who are crushed under the weight of their own self-love, abuse ownership and improperly exercise power.***
- ***Faith and loving unity in Christ calls all to share God's life as His children.***
- ***Council reiterated truth: God intended the earth and everything in it for the use of all humans.***
- ***Common Good – Work – hope, hardship, ambition, and joy are shared — it firmly unites the wills, minds, and hearts of men.***
- ***Balanced Progress – Too many people are suffering. Proper equilibrium needs to be maintained.***
- ***Everyone – The critical state of affairs must be corrected for the better without delay.***
- ***Everyone must lend a hand to the task, particularly those who are by reason of education, office, or authority.***
- ***We cannot proceed to increase the wealth and power of the rich, while we entrench the needy in their poverty; adding to the oppressed. Organized programs are necessary to directing, stimulating, coordinating, supplying, and integrating.***

- ***Temptations – The poorer nations can never be too much on guard against the temptation posed by the wealthy.***
- ***Humanism – True humanism points the way toward God. Man becomes truly man only by passing beyond himself.***
- ***Aid – If a brother or a sister wants of daily food, but you advise/ pray and send them away, extending blessings — how will their needs be met? How could you assist in their circumstances?***
- ***Change is not just a question of eliminating hunger or reducing poverty; it involves building human community, brotherly love, authenticating Christian charity and incorporating spiritual values.***

In 2016, in his letter, let us take a look at what has changed, and honestly know that all, despite his efforts to bring attention to the common man, and to the church, has not changed much. These concerns were noted in 1965. How much time do we need to change, to love, and to reach out, going with the plans of God?

We have had several periods of devastation around the world, and in some ways we have reached out. But the world still needs aid in helping people to work together; loving and giving, upgrading and prospering others. It is far from being reached! The world has had tsunamis, floods, earth quakes, starvation, tornadoes, and much more in many parts of the world, but yet we aid temporarily and still turn our heads and look the other way. Honestly, the problems that exist are everyone's problems, and the problems of the poor will not go away!

In reading all that the Pope IV expressed in the late sixties, we can see that his goal was for all people to live where all needs were met. This letter was written over fifty years ago, and the needs are still relevant today!

"God intended the earth and all that it contains — everything, God intended it for the use of every human person." What God wants is for every one of us and every person on this earth to have the opportunity for a full, human life. That is why God gave us the earth and all that it contains, so that we could have a full human life.

What has happened? We live in a country where we have had protests because there is 1% of the population who have an extraordinary, unbelievable amount of wealth, and 99% who are struggling. Why? Is it due to lack of knowledge in God, lack of knowledge in education? Yes, both. Education, on all levels, equips us to know what direction we should take our lives.

God's Word teaches us how to believe and allows Him to show us our purpose. Purpose-driven individuals have the favor of God on their lives and can live progressively. As progress is made, in return, we can reach back to help others do the same. Truly, to avoid poverty as a country, we must follow the purpose and implement the plan of God to move forward, and always, yes, always redistribute money as needed to the lower income sector in society.

That is a hard saying, but it is part of God's wisdom. If you have more than you need and there is someone who is lacking the necessities of human life, the overflow is not really yours any longer. It belongs to the poor person. It belongs to those who do not have enough. Do we have to change our lifestyle? Perhaps, we may have to change some policies in our country that cause so many to be poor, while the rich become richer, standing financially strong. This is the wisdom of God. It is like a two-edged sword that goes deeply into our being and challenges us and the Word of God, the wisdom of God that becomes the judge of us.

If we follow this wisdom of God, we will not fear, for we will have full human life and we will also be invited by God to everlasting life. The reign of God will be ours if we follow the wisdom, the Word of God, avoid greed in every form, share what we have, and change our ways of life so that everyone has a chance to share in what God has given to all, and not just to a few.

Of course greed as well, can be an issue. Let us take a look at greed and pride.

Chapter 9

Greed and Pride

The opportunity for a full human life is why God gave us the earth, so that we could have the pleasure of life in its fullness, here on the earth. What has happened? **We live in a country where there is 1% who have an extraordinary, unbelievable amount of wealth, and 99% who are struggling. God actually devised a plan so that all will have what they need. It is God's wisdom that will account for a plan to take care of all.**

In looking at why God allows money to be distributed, with some receiving so much more than others, I believe it is a plan to teach us a lesson in self-growth, love for each other, and to learn how to be selfless. The lesson is to see the decline of human suffering, to bring out character, to reach out and make a difference, to aid in bonding, or the growth of humanity, and much more. ... God's plan is to implement the resource, reaching out to the needs of others through people, and showing love to one another.

In order to have a plan that works, we must have a population of individuals in need. On the contrary, we would have individuals who have more than they need. Yes, God supplies to those who lack the necessities of human life. His supply comes from those of wealth as they provide compassion and love to others.

As all should know, greed is not of God. As much as 1% of the population has extraordinary wealth, those of success, God's Chosen Vessels, issued through God's blessings that are poured into their lives. God sets up the imbalance for many reasons, however, anyone who has an excess of the needs of their household should reach back and help the poor or lower income. It is really not a Choice, it is God's plan as the aforementioned scriptures have noted throughout chapters 1-8 of this book.

Should we have to change our lifestyles? Perhaps, we may have to change some policies, maybe change the way we operate in this country. Possibly change the government or the welfare system, or possibly just review what causes so many to be poor, while others become rich. All avenues should be reviewed for options of Change. The change cannot take place in a few months, for it will take years of adjustments. Therefore, God has given responsibility to the believers of the Word to step in and place a wedge between poverty and prosperity. God has a plan and has provided us with the designated purpose to give. All should be mindful, and greed should never take precedence.

Avoid greed in every form, share what we have and change our ways of life so that everyone has a chance to share in what God has given to all, and not just to a few.

All dollars spent should have a purpose, in other words, nothing should be wasted. Money should be used to meet a need or to bless yourself, family or others. This concept is demonstrated in scripture when Jesus fed five thousand, and asked that the scraps of the group be taken up, **(Mark 6:30–44).** *In this case Jesus was distributing food, but in all things Jesus desires that we do not waste or misuse food, money, clothes, land, anything that He willingly provides to us.*

Verses 39–44 reads:

> 39 Then Jesus directed them to have all the people sit down in groups on the green grass.
>
> 40 So they sat down in groups of hundreds and fifties.
>
> 41 Taking the five loaves and the two fish and looking up to heaven, he gave thanks and broke the loaves. Then he gave them to his disciples to distribute to the people. He also divided the two fish among them all.
>
> 42 They all ate and were satisfied,
>
> 43 and the disciples picked up twelve basketfuls of broken pieces of bread and fish.

44 The number of the men who had eaten was five thousand.

God desires no waste, all pieces should be used or given away; to share, give and not hold on or purchase excessively (yes, I am guilty).

What about individuals born with wealth, privileged? Should they FREELY GIVE? Exactly what constitutes greed? Are they demonstrating greed if their desires are to possess multiple quantities of a particular item, such things as shoes, hats, coats, handbags, especially if we are looking at twenty plus? To be honest, each one of us purchases extra, more than we need of certain items, but it gets to a point that we must account for the excess purchases and the needs of others. What would God say about fifty pairs of shoes, or four homes? What would God say about not helping our neighbor if we have over fifty pairs of shoes, or own 5 or more homes, but do not reach out and help our brother. What would God desire that we do? How can we determine when we have enough? When should we stop and sacrifice or just give, because we have **enough to cover our house**.

It is a personal evaluation that we must take the time to review, and determine exactly what we need. Of course the joy of having so much extra is a part of living. It is our assessment, and God only knows Excessive purchases, such as the purchase of extra automobiles, extra homes (multiple homes or homes three or four times the need of the family), having over and above what you need for yourself and your family is considered greed.

1 John 3:17–18, (ESV)

> But if anyone has the world's goods and sees his brother in need, yet closes his heart against him, how does God's love abide in him? Little children, let us not love in word or talk but indeed and in truth.

1 Timothy 5:8, (ESV)

> But if anyone does not provide for his relatives, and especially for members of his household, he has denied the faith and is worse than an unbeliever.

Greed is not of God. As stated earlier, as much as 1% has extraordinary wealth; based on the numbers, up to 99% struggle in one way or another. Success is issued ONLY through God.

In taking a look at greed and the statistics, and looking in a different perspective, many who are privileged, and allow greed to manifest within, have the audacity to joke and look down on others who have less, such as in the act of bullying or out casting. There are people who attend church and are made to feel that their hair, clothes, or level of education is lacking, or they do not have the skills to participate or take on a role with the elite group in the church environment. The leaders tend to isolate themselves and consider themselves in a special group that only includes a certain class of people. To joke even in your own circle, to point fingers, or to laugh at the way an individual pronounces words or has knowledge of the English language, as Christians, is not of God. All are equal, and the same sisters and brothers are equal in God's eyes and should be treated as such.

Many are disabled, but sometimes it is not something someone can pick up just by looking at them. Disabilities can be managed, yet individuals still struggle in performing as someone without. The disabled, in many circles, are out casted and labeled. The poor and seniors are all subject to labels due to adjustments needed to sometime produce. This is not of God!

Yes, many are so proud of their accomplishments and expected to be honored:

The Bible provides an example - Nebuchadnezzar

Learn about Nebuchadnezzar:

Nebuchadnezzar, one of history's most powerful kings, learned this lesson the hard way. One day he went for a walk, and as he strolled, he said, "Is not this the great Babylon I have built as the royal residence by my mighty power and for the Glory of my majesty?" (Daniel 4:30).

God's answer was quick and to the point: He took away the king's sanity and drove him outside to eat grass like a cow. Seven years later, when God restored Nebuchadnezzar's sanity, the king no longer exulted in his possessions, but glorified God as sovereign over all, (Daniel 4:34-37).

Nebuchadnezzar's sin was one of pride; he had the illusion that he was self-sufficient. In essence, he felt that he was successful, that all of his **achievements were things that he accomplished on his own.**

PRIDE

LET GO of the phrase - - - "I earned what I have, through my our achievement" It is not of God.

You may have had thoughts, something like "I earned my money. No one gave it to me. I worked for it."

It may be true, yet it is God who created you in the first place and gave you the strength and talent to earn money. Every new day is given freely to you by God.

You may say to yourself, "My power and the strength of my hands have produced this wealth for me." Remember the LORD, your God, for it is He who gives you the ability to produce wealth, and so confirms his covenant, which he swore to your forefathers as it still stands today.

1 Corinthians 4:7 (NASB)

> 7 For who regards you as superior? What do you have that you did not receive? And if you did receive it, why do you boast as if you had not received it?

Matthew 25:31–46, Summation of These Verses

> "When the Son of Man comes in His Glory, and all the angels with Him, then He will sit on his glorious throne. Before Him will be gathered all the nations, and He will separate people one from another as a shepherd separates the sheep from the goats. And He will place the sheep on his right, but the goats on the left. Then the King will say to those on his right, 'Come, you who are blessed by my Father, inherit the kingdom prepared for you from the foundation of the world. For I was hungry and you gave me food, I was thirsty and you gave me drink, I was a stranger and you welcomed me.'"

Pride accompanies ungratefulness.

(Be Thankful)

Let us review and remember just how Nebuchadnezzar continued to take the credit that was not his, but God's. Nebuchadnezzar's sin was one of pride and illusion of self. In essence, he believed that it was all his doing, that he was self-sufficient. In other words, he thought, "Look at what I did, look at what I have accomplished on my own, by myself."

It is okay to find satisfaction in your work, (**Ecclesiastes 2:24**). Just remember to thank God for creating you and giving you the gifts, skills and strength that allow you to succeed.

Below are additional scriptures to help in the journey to encourage and defined how God provides a Word to help us identify our outlook on pride or thankfulness.

1 Chronicles 29:12–15, (KJV)

> 12 Both riches and honour come of thee, and thou reignest over all; and in thine hand is power and might; and in thine hand it is to make great, and to give strength unto all.
>
> 13 Now therefore, our God, we thank thee, and praise thy glorious name.
>
> 14 But who am I, and what is my people, that we should be able to offer so willingly after this sort? for all things come of thee, and of thine own have we given thee.
>
> 15 For we are strangers before thee, and sojourners, as were all our fathers: our days on the earth are as a shadow, and there is none abiding.

James 2:14–17, (KJV)

> 14 What doth it profit, my brethren, though a man say he hath faith, and have not works? can faith save him?
>
> 15 If a brother or sister be naked, and destitute of daily food,

> [16] And one of you say unto them, Depart in peace, be ye warmed and filled; notwithstanding ye give them not those things which are needful to the body; what doth it profit?
>
> [17] Even so faith, if it hath not works, is dead, being alone.

Proverbs 3:1–35, (KJV)

Remember to be thankful as I summarize:

> Do not forget my teaching, but keep my commandments, for length of days/ years of life and peace they will add. Be in steadfast love and faithfulness; bind them around your neck; write them on your heart. You will find favor in the sight of God. Trust in the Lord with all your heart, and do not lean on your own understanding.

(Treasure God and do not store your treasures on earth.)

Often we believe that the things are really ours. Our attitudes can get our hearts. We need to replace God's truth: God owns it, we must believe and live accordingly.

Talents and/or Gifts – were issued to Glorify God, and all talents earning should be subjective to manifest God on earth. We should freely give, as we are reciprocals of monies to distribute to others who might not have the ability to reach high income levels. There are many individuals who cannot grasp information or learn to a level of high reproduction. Many have the gift to grasp information and can teach skills such as electronics, computers or medical. Specialized skills, for some, are limited. God creates all to establish His Glory, whether there exists, bi-polar, blindness or paraplegic; many at times have a need for financial support.

Seriously, it is not for anyone to judge, but to help in the ways that we see will prosper and aid in the needs of such individuals. All are challenged and must grow into the individuals that God has formed. Yes, a role that God enriches and has chosen to create a variety of people for His Glory for His plan. God provides all opportunities and opens every door; we are not the ones who hold the key to OUR success. God promotes. God provides the talent, and God provides the skills. He will give us the favor so that we will be the ones, the chosen vessels, for a part in a play or the job that we so desire to have. Every opportunity and every winning accomplishment comes from Him, through Him, and by Him.

When successful individuals accept the realization that despite self, the gifts/ talents that are naturally a part of us, were ALL given to us by God, each gift is His that He issued, and that can be given or taken away. Modesty is a must, and to humble oneself is of great pleasure in the eyes of God.

Proverbs 11:28

> 28Those who trust in their **riches** will fall, but the righteous will thrive like a green leaf.

Chapter 10

Sojourn

Earth is God's land. All will return to the Father at the end of time. Armageddon, which every Christian is well aware, as noted in prophecy as expected, the earth and the people, as we know it today, will no longer exist.

All that exists on the earth today will one day be left behind. No one will take the land, auto, job, or home here on earth with them, as God will eventually reclaim the earth out of the hands of the unGodly. Our eternal home, our bodies and our needs, who knows exactly what we will require, meaning our final eternal body and our role on earth or in heaven will not be under our control. Therefore our earthly possessions; will there be a need? So why should we hold on SO tight to possessions of this world? Yes, we should save an inheritance for our children and grandchild, should the world still exist. We should plan and still allow special funds to be set aside and give designated excesses earning, to ones in need? Yes many have to find ways to hold on to money, that the government tax, because of excess. Why not invest in someone, one who needs, someone else's advancement, possibly in their education, in their business, in their means of transportation, or in their need for food, clothes, ministry or just a simple couple hundred dollar cash advance. That could mean the world to someone's success.

Why hold on to thousands of dollars in the bank, when predetermined sums of money can and will be a blessing to poverty-stricken individuals or family who have a yearly income of less than twenty-five thousand, or thirty thousand dollars, depending on family size? Anyone with a tax statement that reflects high levels of personal income per family member, a gracious gift of giving can be managed. Yes, an extraordinary income, God expects blessings to flow to others, and giving is a commandment.

Chose to be the vessel, in this book God desires that awareness is brought to the forefront. Not to pinpoint anyone, but God has summoned a call to look, watch, and discern where finances are needed, to help, invest or teach an individual to reach a level of increase as a demonstration of love.

To help locate a job, hire or recommend an individual for a job, or promote, are all acts of service. There are many ways, but to reach out and get involved as to increase a family in need, is all a part of giving. All are acts that God sees and rewards. As we all know, prayer is always good, we must always remember that God works through people, and that designated individual could be YOU.

Do not always look for another source, when in reality you are fully capable of completing a plan to help. To send someone on their way and offer to pray for them when you are the source that they need, God does not place them in your path—just because—God desires that you act or make a move to help.

To pray for them is like saying, *"I see you have a need, but I cannot help. Let me ask God to place someone else or some organization in your path to help you. God did not lead you to me to help you, but to pray and send you to the next prayer warrior. Surely someone will actually answer the petition of prayer and meet the call." Someone should stop and provide the help needed.* Sincerely that is God's Way.

James 2:14–17, (KJV)

> *What good is it, my brothers, if someone says he has faith but does not have works? Can that faith save him? If a brother or sister is poorly clothed and lacking in daily food, and one of you says to them, "Go in peace, be warmed and fulfilled the need," without giving them the things needed for the body, what good is that? So also faith by itself, if it does not have works, is dead. Are you fully capable of completing a plan to help?*

YES!

Giving to others are part of God's plan for all people.

Come as a servant.

God is a God of increase.

God is the provider (your spouse is not the provider).

God takes care of everyone; trust God.

Giving proves that you trust God to provide all your needs.

In Faith, trusting God to see the manifestation of your fruit.

Let us look at 1 Peter 1: 22–23, (KJV)

> 22 Seeing ye have purified your souls in obeying the truth through the Spirit unto unfeigned love of the brethren, see that ye love one another with a pure heart fervently:
>
> 23 Being born again, not of corruptible seed, but of incorruptible, by the word of God, which liveth and abideth forever.

Managing money and the distribution of the money that God has gifted to you, which is strongly looked into by God, if you read the parable in Luke 19:11–26, this parable points out that each is accountable as recipients, for what God has given them to manage. All should invest or manage what is given. Growth and increases should take place and be managed wisely. Needless your accountability is between you and God, the provider, the one who provides the gift of prosperity.

As Christians, as we read the scriptures, assuredly according to the Word, the end times are upon us. As hard times befall upon the earth, many will be in need, and all must take time to help.

Accountability is between you and God as He knows and gives all. The Church, the Deacon, the Bishop, the Pastor, the Minister, anyone in leadership, is not God. If you do not go to church or cannot make a commitment to belong to one home-based church, you still bear the responsibility to help the poor as God supplies excess. You are the vessel, to discern and help, aiding the poor; it is a calling, a commandment. To love and give is God's way. It is part of God's plan, the plan to promote and establish a system that will provide for the poor and ones in need. He designed and created ALL, and He has expectations that He desires to be fulfilled. Tithing, donating, contributing, sponsoring, any method of giving that He has placed on your heart, obedience should be placed on that call. Everyone is accountable.

In summation, to come to the realization that you will not sojourn here on earth under the same income, body, or lifestyle, the possession that is acquired will be left behind. God states do not store up riches or treasures here on earth, (Matthew 6:19–20), but in heaven. Where should you invest or store of YOUR treasures?

Love is the key to reaching out to others, loving ones neighbor as oneself.

Psalm 127:1-2, (KJV)

A song of ascents, Of Solomon.

> 1 Unless the LORD builds the house, the builders' labor is in vain.
>
> Unless the LORD watches over the city, the guards stand watch in vain.
>
> 2 In vain you rise early and stay up late, toiling for food to eat— for he grants sleep to[a] those he loves.

Take note of how humble Jesus lived.

Jesus, who had the power to live an extravagant life, traveled from house to house, not securing a property, but lived a life of low income. He walked and did not desire extraordinary material possessions.

As Jesus has set the example to live and know that God loves all, He lives with sinners of all types and advises that as people, we look past what people have labeled as a sinner. Jesus sojourned among all types of people. As an example, we should look at a way to help individuals to have a place to live and give to those in need. Zacchaeus offered his home to Jesus and freely gave as he felt the need to change, giving to others. Jesus slept and spent the night in the home of Zacchaeus, (Luke 19:11–26).

Luke 19:2–9, (NIV)

Zacchaeus the Tax Collector

19 Jesus entered Jericho and was passing through.

[2] A man was there by the name of Zacchaeus; he was a chief tax collector and was wealthy.

[3] He wanted to see who Jesus was, but because he was short he could not see over the crowd.

[4] So he ran ahead and climbed a sycamore-fig tree to see him, since Jesus was coming that way.

[5] When Jesus reached the spot, he looked up and said to him, "Zacchaeus, come down immediately. I must stay at your house today."

[6] So he came down at once and welcomed him gladly.

[7] All the people saw this and began to mutter, "He has gone to be the guest of a sinner."

[8] But Zacchaeus stood up and said to the Lord, "Look, Lord! Here and now I give half of my possessions to the poor, and if I have cheated anybody out of anything, I will pay back four times the amount."

[9] Jesus said to him, "Today salvation has come to this house, because
this man, too, is a son of Abraham. [10] For the Son of Man came to seek
and to save the lost."

Sojourn-

Place of worship - The Church are the Members

Love – Give – Teach

As we know our homes on earth are temporary; as well the physical church building. The Church is really there congregation, *The People*. Yet the have a physical home, the church building for a place to Worship. Received the word of God. As we sojourn and gather in the different buildings to receive the teachings, we should always remember to offer up tithes, and offerings; the cost of the building; lights, water, and other bills associated with operating the church building, MUST be maintained. The cost should be received through the people attending.

The teaching of the Word of God should come to all who desire to receive, regardless of cost. If God has a Word, or if teaching is offered, special services, special training/topics such as; Spiritual Gifts, How to Hear God's Voice, Marriage, or Discipleship, all are teachings of the Word of God and no one should be turned away due to a cost to attend. If anyone desires to learn, but does not have the extra money to pay for special training, all should be welcome to attend. The Word is God's should always be a received as a gift to any man desiring to receive. Cost should be covered through an offering or the tithes.

If you are associated with a church and desire to learn as much as you can about His Word, you should never be denied based on money. Somehow, something should be worked out so that attendance becomes available, whether you volunteer or complete community service for the church or community, bible learning/spiritual growth should be available. The Word was given freely by God and should be made available to any church member who wants to learn, and at no cost.

Yes, it is understood that special speakers come out to give the Word, and cost is involved. The church should assist with those costs through offerings and tithes previously provided, or if a (low) registration fee is needed, it is acceptable. However, if someone expresses a sincere interest, but does not have the necessary funds, they should not be turned away. Sponsors or a special account should be set to allow for their participation. Donations or an offering basket, for those who can give, could also be an option. However, regardless of money, God's Word and teachings should go forth to all who reach out to receive.

The believers sojourn in the church, it is the home, the holy place of God. It is the place where we go to seek spiritual feeding. God commands that His sheep are fed and He has summoned ministries to complete the task. The door should be open anytime the Word is available. Love and give the Word of God, without fees. The house of God should not forget its purpose, sincerely. To request an offering is acceptable, yet the house of God is considered to be the Temple and the "PLACE TO RECEIVE THE WORD OF GOD." GOD WILL PROVIDE A WAY TO COVER THE COST OF THE MINISTRY. LOVE, LOVE ENOUGH, TO GIVE FREELY. (suggestions only: complete fund raisers, dances, dinners, carnivals, musicals, bake sales, fun activities ... Christian events, extras family events for fun to assist with cost).

CHAPTER 11

LOVE

Commandment - Love your neighbor as you love yourself.

Love God — First

Love yourself — Second

All Below Are Included or defined As Your Neighbor--

- **Love your spouse**
- **Love your children/family**
- **Love friends/associates**

Love everyone "neighbors" ALL ABOVE ARE YOUR SISTER AND BROTHERS IN CHRIST

One way that many have taken the time to demonstrate love is by giving single acts of kindness to individuals that they see on the street or meet in a grocery store, at the beauty salon, or on the job. Giving and supporting someone financially by doing an act of kindness is such a rewarding gesture. God desires that we give, share, provide and enlighten one's day by doing an unexpected deed. This warms hearts and demonstrates the love of God here on earth. Love is the greatest of all the fruits of the Spirit. Love thy neighbor, what a beautiful way to express love. The investment of time and the giving of money are usually so rewarding that we feel honored to serve our fellow man! Yes, God's love expressed through us wins souls!

1Peter 1:17

[17] Honour all men. Love thy brotherhood. Fear God. Honour the king.

LOVE GOD FIRST

Love God and be mindful that there is only ONE true God. Anything that you put money or time into that tends to control your time or money becomes "God" in your life. What you talk about most; worship (adore, like) can all be the god in your life. Most definitely what you spend most of your money on, it does not matter whether it is music, child, wife, auto, a collection of jewels, a purse collection, or even a sports team; ALL can be a god in your life. Believe it or not, envying or adoring a pastor can become to you the God that you worship versus the true creator, Almighty God, the divine creator. No other should be worshiped, for idiots are easily taken and replace as the Holy Creator, the God of truth, therefore be "Caution."

Love your Pastor, Bishop, (man or woman), Leaders of God, but be leery that God always has first place in your life. Your Pastor, Minister, man or lady of God, is not God in any respect. Honoring them or worshiping them can reach the level of a godly adoration, it can become a thin line between how and why you show honor to them, stand on "their" every word without self-study of biblical truths. As well as following without seeking that it is God's direction for your life. Always ask God to discern or provide revelation on task, direction or giving to certain programs.

If you find yourself always speaking about the greatness of you pastor, and you donate money because the pastor has asked to causes that always require a new collection or organization that is collecting additional monies from the congregation consistently. Make wise choices when you giving to God or your pastor, outside the standard tithe. Question truly why you are volunteering or extending time, donating items, etc...? Is it sincerely all about God in your heart and spirit, or is it to impress the leaders of the ministry? Are you serving God or the men that applauds you for the commitment that you give to the church? If you were never recognized for your participation or no one knew that you gave, would you still give? **Give in secret**, because God will always know what you have done and reward you. You are a vessel for God!

Search and keep a check of your perspective of anything that could be a god in your life. It may be money, it may be a sports team, or maintaining your beauty (nails, hair, make-up, clothes). Yet you may not understand that many things that you love may cross the line. To worship people, self, work, pro-teams or music, can get to a level that is unbalanced, becoming a god in your life. No man should be worshipped or place on a pedestal. The God of Abraham, Isaac, and Jacob is the only God of Worship. Love thou God first is the first Commandment.

Deuteronomy 6:4–6, (KJV)

> 4 Hear, O Israel: The LORD our God is one LORD:
>
> 5 And thou shalt love the LORD thy God with all thine heart, and with all thy soul, and with all thy might.
>
> 6 And these words, which I command thee this day, shall be in thine heart:
>
> As well, we should love God first and our neighbors foremost—(2nd) -

Deuteronomy 7:9, (KJV)

> 9 Know therefore that the LORD thy God, he is God, the faithful God, which keepeth covenant and mercy with them that love him and keep his commandments to a thousand generations;

God calls for us to know who we are in HIM, knowing that He loves us immensely. Yet we must know how to balance and love others, and all that He has given us starts the escalation of the gifts inspired through God in us. God has continued to give to our lives, adding talents, finances, spouse, child/children, mastery of school/work/church; yes, divine favor, the ability to walk, to see, to speak, and to hear. God has, at different times, indeed granted favor as our blessings overflow.

John 15:13–16, (KJV)

> 13 Greater love hath no man than this, that a man lay down his life for his friends.

14 Ye are my friends, if ye do whatsoever I command you.

15 Henceforth I call you not servants; for the servant knoweth not what his lord doeth: but I have called you friends; for all things that I have heard of my Father I have made known unto you.

16 Ye have not chosen me, but I have chosen you, and ordained you, that ye should go and bring forth fruit, and that your fruit should remain: that whatsoever ye shall ask of the Father in my name, he may give it you.

It is a choice, to love, to give, and sacrifice for the life of others. Jesus called the believers his Friends. God loved all and as He has called, He has ordained too. As "Chosen Vessels" God has equipped and prepared man to move forth in love.

As the Bible indicates in 1 Corinth 13: Love never fails:

1 Corinthians 13:2–8 and 13, (NIV)

13 If I speak in the tongues[a] of men or of angels, but do not have love, I am only a resounding gong or a clanging cymbal.

2 If I have the gift of prophecy and can fathom all mysteries and all knowledge, and if I have a faith that can move mountains, but do not have love, I am nothing.

3 If I give all I possess to the poor and give over my body to hardship that I may boast,[b] but do not have love, I gain nothing.

4 Love is patient, love is kind. It does not envy, it does not boast, it is not proud.

5 It does not dishonor others, it is not self-seeking, it is not easily angered, it keeps no record of wrongs.

> [6] Love does not delight in evil but rejoices with the truth.
>
> [7] It always protects, always trusts, always hopes, always perseveres.
>
> [8] Love never fails.

And

> [13] And now these three remain: faith, hope and love. But the greatest of these is love.

All should strive to love unconditionally and work toward loving self and others as God indicates in the first and second commandments. In loving as God has instructed, all the other commandments will be present in our lives. Jesus was a perfect example of such love.

Therefore, if we have any excess of property, cars, homes, or wealth, and we see our brother with needs, we should, as the commandment states, Love them and Give. As the second coming of Christ approaches, how can one look and not give?

How can we see our brother in need and not provide? How do we as people have the audacity to keep the extra that God has blessed us with financially, and call ALL THINGS "HIS", YET WE LABEL IT "MINE", and hold on to it without helping our fellow man (our neighbor)? Many have issues due to unjust, biases, hurt, shame, closed doors, education, mental dilemmas, social standards, forgiveness, divorce, and sexual choices. These are the roots of most fallen financial cycles, which starts the flow of problems, causing an ongoing cycle. God speaks against each one of these issues, WHEN THE ACT OF LOVE CONQUERS ALL.

How do we stand as a united nation, helping others from other countries, but do not clean up our country? Giving to anyone anywhere is a good thing. No one desires to hold up signs and ask for help (as we see on street corners, people asking for help). Are we blind to the people around us? Start in your communities.

Poverty can start with missing a check or two, and from that point it escalates and the cycle is in motion. Yes, without help, anyone who lives from check to check can be one under a bridge. If we can look and see, we can stop the advancement well before individuals become homeless. Look, give what you can, time, money or education. Everyone has something to give as love should prompt us to give. WE MUST TEACH AS AN ACT OF LOVE. TO FEED IS AN ACT OF LOVE, TO SPEND TIME IS AN ACT OF LOVE, AND TO LISTEN IS AN ACT OF LOVE. MUST I SAY, TO "CLEANSE" IS AN ACT OF LOVE.

Let us not look away, but look ahead and look deeply. Many do not speak or tell, but there is evidence in the eyes, voice, and spirit of our fellow man. Look for it. It is there, it exist.

In reading scriptures, God tells us not to store up material possessions here on earth, but look for heavenly things.

Colossians 3:2–4, (KJV)

> 3 If ye then be risen with Christ, seek those things which are above, where Christ sitteth on the right hand of God.
>
> 2 Set your affection on things above, not on things on the earth.
>
> 3 For ye are dead, and your life is hid with Christ in God.
>
> 4 When Christ, who is our life, shall appear, then shall ye also appear with him in glory.

As well, in the scripture below, the Word gives direction on giving to others. God knows everything and knows what we can or cannot do. God gives and expects that our perspective for the poor is open-minded enough to know that it is given unto us so as to help others as needed.

Matthew 5:42, (KJV)

> 42 Give to him that asketh thee, and from him that would borrow of thee turn not thou away.

Col 3:12–15, (KJV)

> [12] Put on therefore, as the elect of God, holy and beloved, bowels of mercies, kindness, humbleness of mind, meekness, longsuffering;
>
> [13] Forbearing one another, and forgiving one another, if any man have a quarrel against any: even as Christ forgave you, so also do ye.
>
> [14] And above all these things put on charity, which is the bond of perfectness.
>
> [15] And let the peace of God rule in your hearts, to which also ye are called in one body; and be ye thankful.

The NIV – states in verse 14 of the same book.

> *[14] And over all these* ***virtues put on love, which binds them all together in perfect unity****.*

Always give thanks to God, the creator of all things.

Speak adoration for the creator for all that He has created; from the flowers, the multiple colors, to the world around us, of the combination of earth and rocks, trees and bushes, birds and people. Look at all the different types of creation; people of distinct features, colors, hair types, eyes, nose, and lips. Yes, all are beautifully created. Acknowledge God's work, the almighty creator of all things and the power to see, hear, and produce anything and All things.

Remember the promise of God in Luke.

Luke 6:38, (NIV)

> [38] Give, and it will be given to you. A good measure, pressed down, shaken together and running over, will be poured into your lap. For with the measure you use, it will be measured to you."

God is omnipresent and omnipotent and, Can Do All Things. The Father of the

Earth—the Father of the Universe—No one can take the Glory for His magnificent Work.

God moves on your behalf. You have His grace and His unconditional love always.

His Word speaks as we read.

Deuteronomy 10:14, (KJV)

> 14 Behold, the heaven and the heaven of heavens is the LORD's thy God, the earth also, with all that therein is.

Marriage as many debate.

When it comes to marriage, note that it is one money source.

Even in marriage, no one of the two bounded together are owners of the house, car, boat, or the children. ALL belong to God. God blesses the Union and the blessings extend to the children. The money and all items are God's, which permits both parties to share. As both, upon marriage, become one, and the gift of financial growth and material growth belongs to the God, the "ONE" Union shares in the gift that God supplies to the Union. The marriage represents a household of the married couple and the minor children. The gift of giving falls under that household, denoted as "One," and the money earned when it comes to tithing, as "One," when the gift of giving is administrated.

An important principle to keep firmly in mind is to understand whose money we are talking about. The union means that the money becomes both, united as a total sum; ONE, not separate. All are stewards, the couple gives as one, as God summons, united as stewards of money that God provides to the household.

THE WASHING -

To **Love** one another—As Jesus set the example.

Jesus showed the disciples an example of love during the Last Supper, by washing the feet of each disciple. The demonstration of love, as it is shown with the washing, teaches all how to show humility and to give love to others. Submit by showing love to our fellow man, as Jesus came to love and serve, not to be served.

The **Servant Vessel**, the vessel of submitting one to another, the desire to give only to the ones who we know is not valid. The love that we show our neighbor, the love that we demonstrate represents God and the Greatness that cannot be expressed in any other way than to give of one's self. To have possessions or the desire to own many possessions are in vain, and not of loving character.

As many people are starving, and without shoes, clothes, or shelter, how should we act or respond? How should we look at our needs compared to a hungry child or a family going from one house to the next, due to the lack of housing? How do we justify? How do we close our eyes to what is visible?

Jesus stated that he was **Master and Lord; the Great, "I AM."** Yet, Jesus was a servant and washed the feet of the disciples, desiring that all hold this attitude towards serving and giving. LOVE–LOVE–LOVE, as we are summoned to **Give as Chosen Vessels**.

In Matthew 13: 4–16, (KJV)—Jesus professes a servant ship attitude. Below are three verses that express 14-16 (KJV)

Matthew 13:14–16, (KJV)

> 14 If I then, your Lord and Master, have washed your feet; ye also ought to wash one another's feet.
>
> 15 For I have given you an example, that ye should do as I have done to you.
>
> 16 Verily, verily, I say unto you, The servant is not greater than his lord; neither he that is sent greater than he that sent him.

Hardship of an individual should never be overlooked. The problem is not just an individual problem; it is a community and/or church problem. Take the time to wash the feet of your fellow man. It does not mean always to literally wash feet, but to extend help and love, and the attitude of servant ship to all that are placed in our path. God does place divine encounters before us every day. Our hearts/spirits have to be visually in tune to see. Seek, look, and acknowledge.

Chapter 12

Chosen, The "Chosen Vessel" Of God

God asks of us to love Him by keeping his commandments, to love His church (the people); not just the leaders. Never lose perspective by loving and honoring the leaders of the church before God. Pastors, Bishops, Deacons should receive their respect, but always remember that God is the provider and the one who anoints, for He should receive all of our praise. Worship belongs to the Great "I AM."

All is provided through the Father of all creation. Tithes should be given, but distribution of additional money should be given to individuals or organizations that you can see has a need. God leads and guides us in making those decisions. As the end times approach, and as Christians representing God's Kingdom, all should meet the needs of the poor, taking care of one another. Remember, blessings are given as faithful servants, as the chosen vessel. God holds accountable to ones that He has gifted/given/provided financial favor, so as to enhance lives and place in the hands a financial blessing, of all who has a need.

As the Chosen Vessel, step-by-step, we reach out to a level of perfecting the divine touch of God. Teach as we love and manifest the ability to discern the needs of people. As an act of stewardship in love and grace, the hand of God has miraculously supplied a way for many, though, His Chosen Vessels. As the Chosen Vessel all should embrace those who are "Poverty Stricken" and "Victoriously" make a substantial difference. God has a plan that no one lacks, and that all needs are met.

*****As Poverty strikes, purpose are defined, knowledge/ wisdom is gained; it in turn becomes the raw essence of prosperity.*****

Everything belongs to God. We are the Chosen Vessels that God filters resources through. Believe me, it is not foreign, and we must come to the consensus that we are His, His creation, and all that we do and accomplish is part of the creative work, the craftsmanship of the heavenly Father. As vessels, we honor the Father in giving. Yes, some would like to think of our money and our possessions as solely ours, to do as we please, yet the Bible makes it clear that God owns everything. All things were created for His Glory. (Colossians 1:16) Awe, for the majestic Glory of God!

A PRAYER FOR THE FINANCIAL DISHEARTED

If you seek financial help, below is a simple prayer you can pray two to three times daily for God to Lift YOU out of your circumstances.

Heavenly Father, I praise You for my life and all the blessings that You have provided me.

I praise You for this day and every day. You are the Lord of Lords and the King of Kings.

You are Powerful and Majestic, All Knowing and Omni Present.

I come to You in prayer, as Your Word states; "you have not, because you ask not."

Father, today I ask that You dismiss the spirit of poverty from my house.

My house will serve and Glorify You as we strive to prosper here on earth.

I declare and decree from this day forward, that I will work toward financial security, financial freedom.

I take authority over any hindering spirits of poverty and bind them, in the mighty name of "Jesus."

For my Lord, You are my provider, my Jehovah-Jireh. I believe and speak abundance over my house, in the name of Jesus.

I am blessed going in and blessed coming out!

As I am blessed, I desire to add financial blessings to the House of God and to others.

I profess that the door of prosper will open and financial treasures released.

I speak into existence the spirit of prosperity.

In the Name of Jesus!

With thanksgiving, I praise You for my financial blessing.

In Christ Jesus Name,

--- Amen ---

About the Author

The Author S. R. Sampson is a student at Liberty University, studying Biblical Studies. Originally from Dallas, Texas and currently residing in the state of Georgia.

Printed in the United States
By Bookmasters